SN57 FBB

FAST CARS

Discover the world's fastest supercars

igloobooks

igloobooks

Published in 2017
by Igloo Books Ltd
Cottage Farm
Sywell
NN6 0BJ
www.igloobooks.com

HUN001 0817
4 6 8 10 9 7 5 3
ISBN 978-1-78557-434-4

Front and back cover images: © Drive Images / Alamy Stock Photo

Cover designed by Charles Wood-Penn
Edited by Caroline Icke

Written by Robin Brown

Printed and manufactured in China

CONTENTS

INTRODUCTION

It's extraordinary that the top speed of the world's fastest production car is the best part of 200mph faster than many legal speed limits of Western roads. For many owners of the world's most powerful supercars and hypercars the chance to make the most of their wheels might only come rarely - at the track or a journey through Germany, with its limitless Autobahnen.

It begs the questions as to why these cars even exist, why people buy them and why they're so desirable. For car manufacturers there exist huge PR benefits to building the fastest car in the world, but the technological advances that building such a car - and overcoming the accompanying obstacles - brings are significant too. As with motorsports, the advances in technology gleaned through producing these wickedly fast machines often filters down into high-volume road cars.

But there's a common reason as to why car-makers and car-buyers are entranced by speed: the simple love of cars and the desire to push the envelope. Some manufacturers eschew raw speed - prioritising driving dynamics, luxury or a combination of several factors. Yet Bugatti, SSC, Koenigsegg and others continue to battle it out for the crown of the fastest car in the world. Why? For the same reasons given by Mallory in retort to why climbing Everest was so important. Meeting the challenge - beating it, and achieving what was previously thought impossible.

Building a car that can travel at speed of over 250mph – much faster than a Formula One car – is an extraordinary technical challenge. Power required increases exponentially at speeds above 200mph thanks to aerodynamic drag.

So too does cooling and heat venting. Airflow over and under the car becomes a delicate balance between slipperiness and preventing the car from taking off. Fuel economy plummets to the point that miles per gallon are registered in barely whole numbers. And tyres operate at the very limits of the forces they can withstand.

The Veyron has, essentially, two V8 engines in tandem, with 16 cylinders and four turbochargers. Most cars have one radiator, the Veyron has 12. Its fuel pump capacity is eight times greater than most cars and it consumes the same amount of air in one minute as the air consumed by a man in four days.

That these fastest cars can hit those speeds while offering music players, satellite navigation, climate control and adjustable seats – all the creature comforts of an executive sedan – is so incredible it's almost laughable.

In their way these fastest cars in the world are less comparable to everyday road cars than they are to the flagships of modern speed, technology, inventiveness. The Flying Scotsman. Bluebird. Concorde. Yet they also represent one of the fundamental challenges that define us as a race. To be higher, faster, stronger. There are very good reasons to build the fastest car in the world, but the one that unites those who make cars and those who admire them is one of the most simple instincts; the desire to go faster.

FAST CARS
180–190
MPH

PORSCHE 911
CARRERA 4S

Porsche surprised everyone with the
911 Carrera 4S - a supercar that added
all-wheel drive to the 911 template.

While that may raise eyebrows - the 911's reputation as something of an untamed rear-wheel drive beast lends itself to expressive driving - there have been 911s in the past that send power to all four wheels.

The 911's unusual rear-mounted engine set-up makes for a singular challenge for drivers: that's the thrill of taming the Porsche supercar, but it poses unique challenges too - the spectre of oversteer haunting the inexperienced driver.

The obvious benefit of all-wheel drive is that torque is sent to all four wheels and, with almost 400bhp on tap, that's not a bad thing. In slippery conditions the all-wheel drive set up - capable of sending 100% of power to the front axle - offers significant security.

While that might suggest that the Carrera 4S has its edges smoothed off, this is still a supercar that can hit almost 190mph and sprints to 62mph in 4.5 seconds.

That's courtesy of a 394bhp 3.8-litre flat six engine through a slick seven-speed double-clutch autobox that aids fast starts, plus plenty of low-down pull from 440Nm of torque. Sport and Sport Plus setting firm up the suspension and throttle responses - as well as boosting the engine's throaty soundtrack.

The 911 has often been called the thinking man's supercar; with the 4S it could also be called the everyday supercar. Only this daily drive tops out at a startling 185 mph.

SPECIFICATION

MANUFACTURE DATE	2012	ENGINE	3.8-litre flat-six petrol
WIDTH	1,852 mm	TRANSMISSION	Six-speed manual
HEIGHT	1,303 mm	0-62 MPH	4.5 seconds
LENGTH	4,491 mm	POWER OUTPUT	394 / bhp
MAXIMUM TORQUE	440 / nm	BRAKES	4-piston, aluminium fixed monobloc calipers with, cross-drilled, ventilated discs
MAXIMUM SPEED	185 mph	SUSPENSION	McPherson strut suspension at front LSA multi-link at rear

AUDI
R8 V8

Audi is no stranger to All-Wheel Drive – it is, after all, the creator of the iconic Quattro – so it should come as no surprise that this manufacturer's supercar has all four wheels powered.

The mid-engined Audi R8 won plaudits for being a practical and versatile supercar, built using some components from the Lamborghini Gallardo, but that doesn't dull the car's mighty power.

Now with either a six-speed manual or S tronic twin-clutch gearbox, the R8's beating heart is a mid-mounted 4.2-litre V8 petrol engine – matching huge power and traction to super-fast gear changes. It's a booming soundtrack from the eight-cylinder engine when the needle approaches the red line.

The R8 pulls like a train throughout the rev range thanks to closely-spaced gears, while the optional S tronic semi-auto offers lightning quick shifts.

The extra grip afforded by the four-wheel drive brings extra safety, but also performance in difficult conditions and staggering stickiness, despite the 430Nm of torque on tap.

However there's also good refinement and everyday usability, though car buffs may notice some similarities in the cabin to less exotic cars in the Audi range. While that may dismay some, with a price tag around £90,000, it's only the most superficial comparison to any of the other cars bearing the four circles on the grille.

SPECIFICATION

MANUFACTURE DATE	2006	ENGINE	4.2-litre V8 petrol
WIDTH	2,029 mm	TRANSMISSION	Six-speed manual
HEIGHT	1,252 mm	0-62 MPH	4.6 seconds
LENGTH	4,431 mm	POWER OUTPUT	430 / bhp
MAXIMUM TORQUE	430 / nm	BRAKES	Wave brake discs, internally ventilated, 8-piston brake calipers at front; 4-piston at rear
MAXIMUM SPEED	187 mph	SUSPENSION	Sports suspension with dynamically tuned spring and damper combination

While the car's exotic looks might give the edge on design, the R8 also has good interior space and is well-heeled for a car that can legitimately be driven around a track – including all the bells and whistles that a driver might expect to see in an executive car.

It doesn't dent pure driving pleasure, however – the Audi supercar is every bit as agile as you'd expect from a sports car. There's very little body roll when cornering, but the suspension doesn't feel overly firm. Magnetic ride dampers can even be selected with the car, giving an even better combination of driving dynamics and ride comfort.

It's just another example of the balance between track-day exuberance and everyday usability that characterises this fine supercar from Audi.

MOSLER
MT900S

Transported straight from the track – and with only a few minimal adjustments from a genuine racer – the Mosler MT900S is lightweight and very fast. Topping out at 190mph, the Mosler gets very fast extremely quickly – to 60mph in a frightening 3.1 seconds, breaking the 100mph barrier in 6.6 seconds.

The MT900S uses a supercharged 5.7-litre V8 from Chevrolet, which puts out 435bhp in a carbon-aluminium set-up. This lack of weight is the secret to the Mosler's eye-watering acceleration – the power-to-weight ratio approaches an impressive 500bhp-per-ton.

American-based Mosler Automotive is owned by Warren Mosler, a financial guru with a serious passion for things fast and four-wheeled. The transmission is a Porsche 911 GT3-sourced six-speed gearbox or the Hewland six-speed sequential 'box that's a remnant from the track car.

The 435bhp 5.7-litre Corvette-sourced V8 engine develops maximum power at 5,800 rpm and there's also 542Nm of torque on tap that's accessible at ferociously short notice.

As a result there's very little that's polite or refined about the Mosler. The flipside of owning a stripped-out racer is that there are no mod cons, the engine noise intrudes massively into the cockpit and the cabin is basic. Entry into the car is via gullwing doors over a thick sill; the driver sits very low down in the cockpit too.

Steering is remarkably direct but very heavy – another nod to the Mosler's heritage – and the

suspension, while not bad for a race car, is fairly stiff, meaning that the MT900S is far from ideal for a jaunt to the shops.

However, for a car that mixes the best of the track with the usability that means it can be used on the road, the Mosler is a strong, blisteringly quick, package.

SPECIFICATION

MANUFACTURE DATE	2005	**ENGINE**	5.7-litre LS6 V-8
WIDTH	1,998 mm	**TRANSMISSION**	Six-speed manual
HEIGHT	1,041 mm	**0-62 MPH**	3.1 seconds
LENGTH	4,730 mm	**POWER OUTPUT**	435 / bhp @ 5,800 rpm
MAXIMUM TORQUE	542 / nm @ 4,800 rpm	**BRAKES** AP 6-piston front calipers, 378mm ventilated front disc AP 4-piston rear calipers, 355mm ventilated rear disc	
MAXIMUM SPEED	190 mph	**SUSPENSION**	Double wishbones at front and rear

CORVETTE
Z06

Take the endurance racing favourite Chevrolet Corvette C6-R and add a stereo, leather seats and air con. What do you have? Pretty much the Z06 – a de facto track-car with just enough to make the transition to the road viable.

Still, the Z06 is as close to the original as possible; Chevrolet claims that the car can be taken racing without a single tweak to the set-up. With swathes of aluminium, carbon fibre, a magnesium-alloy roof and even balsa wood that's no surprise. That the Corvette weighs a frankly ridiculous 1419kg – 68kg lighter than a standard C6 – couldn't fail to elicit an appreciative whistle however.

The long-lived, all-aluminium Chevrolet V8 develops 512bhp at 7000rpm and 636Nm of torque – figures that indicate that every spare horse and Newton Meter has been wrung out of the Chevy small-block.

The six-speed transmission and the uprated limited-slip differential are in place to keep all of that power and twist in check – while an exhaust valve boosts the soundtrack above 3500rpm, just in case there's any doubt about the intent behind this car.

Magnetic Selective Ride Control comes with Performance Traction Management that allows five different levels of traction management: Wet, Dry, Sport, Sport II and Race, with progressively less interference from the traction system.

The Z06 sprints to 60mph in 3.9 seconds so it's no surprise that the car comes with an improved limited-slip differential, traction control and massive six-piston racing brake calipers on the front. There's plenty to keep all that power and torque in check, but the Corvette can be driven in reasonably sedate fashion too – long gearing ensures that the car can cruise comfortably at 50mph in sixth gear.

Aside from some aerodynamics and a wider rear quarter, there's little to suggest that the Z06 isn't the standard C6. And there's a good ride, luggage space and a reasonably comfortable cabin too, making the Z06 a potential daily drive.

It is best suited for tight roads, where it excels with the right sort of handling. Despite its creature comforts, the Z06 is fundamentally a supercar, its track-day origins making it a fearsome Ferrari- and Porsche-bothering road car.

SPECIFICATION

MANUFACTURE DATE	2004-13	**ENGINE**	7.0-litre V8
WIDTH	1,844 mm	**TRANSMISSION**	Six-speed auto
HEIGHT	1,245 mm	**0-62 MPH**	3.9 seconds
LENGTH	4,435 mm	**POWER OUTPUT**	512 / bhp
MAXIMUM TORQUE	636 / nm	**BRAKES**	6 piston calipers front, 4 at rear
MAXIMUM SPEED	190 mph	**SUSPENSION**	Double-wishbone with Magnetic Ride Control shocks and aluminium control arms

ASTON MARTIN
VANTAGE V12

Adding a V12 to the compact Vantage coupé – also available as a roadster – means an inevitable boost in power, torque and performance over the standard Vantage. The free-revving 510bhp 6.0-litre V12 is the fastest Vantage, capable of 190mph in sixth gear at the red line of 6800rpm through a manual stick shifter, while 60mph takes 4.2 seconds courtesy of peak torque of 570Nm at 5750rpm – all of that torque means the V12 Vantage is easy to drive in several gears at any one time.

The car boasts carbon-ceramic brakes and forged aluminium wheels to keep additional weight in check – as a result the V12 Vantage weighs only 50kg more than the V8, while the car's weight distribution is a near-perfect 49:51 front-to back.

A lower and firmer chassis boosts handling, while a Sport button sharpens throttle response and boosts the throaty roar of the V12. Hitting the Sport button while driving immediately firms up responses to the extent that the car's physical character changes noticeably.

A new rear spring design and a modified damper set-up have been introduced to the car to handle the car's power, though traction control smooths out the worst excesses. Steering is direct and the ride is reasonably firm but supple. Meanwhile standard carbon-ceramic brakes ensure that stopping isn't problematic.

KX10 G

ASTON MARTIN CV35 0DB

A gaping grille and low front splitter are additions to the Vantage template, while a carbon fibre rear diffuser, bonnet vents and side sills all work to redirect air around – and vent it from – the car. While functional, these visual flourishes give the Vantage an angry look that's completely in keeping with the car's nature.

The Vantage in V8 format is hardly serene, yet the addition of a V12 pushes the envelope further; acceleration feels brutish while the engine note is pitched somewhere between thrilling and frightening.

Nevertheless, Aston's reputation for building high-quality cars means that the car's fit and finish is superb, while a 300-litre boot makes the car unusually versatile and practical – this is one supercar that you can take to the golf club.

Proof that the manufacturer can do more than big, languidly powerful grand tourers, the V12 Vantage is simply a classic example of Aston Martin matching style and huge performance.

SPECIFICATION

MANUFACTURE DATE	2007	**ENGINE**	V12, 5,935cc
WIDTH	1,865 mm	**TRANSMISSION**	Six-speed manual, rear-wheel drive, limited-slip diff, DSC
HEIGHT	1,241 mm	**0-62 MPH**	4.2 seconds
LENGTH	4,385 mm	**POWER OUTPUT**	510/ bhp @ 6500 rpm
MAXIMUM TORQUE	570 / nm @ 5750 rpm	**BRAKES**	Ventilated and cross-drilled carbon-ceramic discs 398mm front, 360mm rear
MAXIMUM SPEED	190 mph	**SUSPENSION**	Double-wishbone, coil springs, dampers, anti-roll bar. LSA multi-link at rear

ASTON MARTIN
DB9

The iconic DB9 is a grand tourer that pays tribute to former owner Dave Brown, with all the hallmarks of an Aston Martin – it's cool, elegant and sleek. But it can also travel at speeds nearing 200mph.

The DB9's 6.0-litre V12 develops 470bhp, but it's the 600Nm of torque and its impressive pull from low revs that set the DB9 apart as something special. It takes 4.8 seconds to hit 60mph and the top speed is 190mph – however it's the way that power is transmitted so smoothly through either a six-speed manual or six-speed automatic Touchtronic gearbox, which can be controlled using wheel-mounted paddles for changing gear.

The Aston Martin 2+2 is most at home on smooth, flat A-roads, where it is poised and has glue-like grip going around corners, but it's refined at even high speeds, making it perfect for long punts down motorways, freeways or the Autobahn. The Volante version loses the roof but there's no accompanying drop in performance.

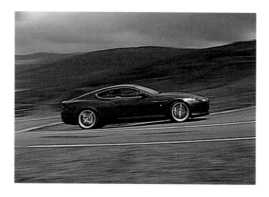

The DB9 is refined and poised – as the James Bond connection demands – and inside, the car has more toys than Q might pack it with. Alongside the usual navigation and media additions there's a raft of safety kit from Volvo (the only clue that the DB9 shares some limited similarities with its then-stablemates Ford, Volvo, Jaguar and Land Rover) and even a tracker so that police can pick up the car should it be acquired by bad guys, though sadly no ejector seat.

The Aston Martin DB9 is a potent combination of power and elegance – combining long range touring ability and fine sports car handling. As such, the latest Dave Brown is classic Aston Martin.

SPECIFICATION

MANUFACTURE DATE	2008-2012	ENGINE	748-valve 6.0-litre petrol V12
WIDTH	1,017 mm	TRANSMISSION	Six-speed manual or touchtronic
HEIGHT	1,270 mm	0-62 MPH	4.6 seconds
LENGTH	4,710 mm	POWER OUTPUT	470 / bhp
MAXIMUM TORQUE	600 / nm	BRAKES	Brembo carbon-ceramic brakes
MAXIMUM SPEED	190 mph	SUSPENSION	All-round independent double-wishbone suspension

FAST CARS
190–200
MPH

CADILLAC
CTS-V
COUPE

The Cadillac CTS-V is something of a rarity among ultra performance cars. With its origins in the CTS executive sedan, this souped-up coupé benefits from a 6.2-litre petrol engine borrowed from the Corvette ZR1.

That means enormous power of 564bhp at 6100rpm and torque figures of 745Nm at 3800rpm and a top speed of 191mph – figures that put it at the top of the tree compared to similar-sized sedans. In fact, with a Nordschleife time of under eight seconds, the CTS-V Coupé was officially the fastest production car of its segment in the world until very recently.

The Cadillac is fast off the mark too, with a 60mph sprint time of 3.9 seconds courtesy of a rasping V8 sending power to the rear wheels. The engine's eight cylinders are only served by two valves, with all that extra poke coming from a big supercharger.

While the CTS-V isn't optimised for twisty roads like its European rivals from BMW, Audi and Mercedes, the ride comfort is superb, the Cadillac's suspension smoothing out ruts and bumps.

Magnetic ride dampers mean the car can be driven in a number of suspension modes, depending on conditions and the driver's priorities. Sport mode hangs onto gear longer with the automatic, meaning the gearbox only shifts up when the red line is approaching. In manual models General Motors' Stabilitrak stability control can be set to Competitive to firm up responses.

Bold, bulky styling marks out the Caddy as an American car through and through and the interior is the match, with leather or Recaro sports seats available. It's packed with equipment, including leather seats, an advanced stereo system with both CD and MP3 connectivity, parking sensors, cruise control, climate control and a built-in satnav system – a rare level of specification for such a performance-oriented car.

The idea of a 'hot' Cadillac seems slightly counter-intuitive, but the fast sedan matches the mod cons and comfort that drivers demand from sports sedans and offers phenomenal power and speed. A new version, with futuristic styling and an improved cabin, was out in 2013, but discontinued in 2015.

SPECIFICATION

MANUFACTURE DATE	2011	ENGINE	V8, 16-valve, 6162cc
WIDTH	1,883 mm	TRANSMISSION	Six-speed manual
HEIGHT	1,422 mm	0-62 MPH	4.0 seconds
LENGTH	4,808 mm	POWER OUTPUT	564 / bhp
MAXIMUM TORQUE	747 / nm	BRAKES	Brembo carbon
MAXIMUM SPEED	191 mph	SUSPENSION	Driver-selectable dual-mode Magnetic Ride Control suspension system

ASTON MARTIN
DBS V12

Look familiar? If you're wondering where you might have seen the Aston Martin DBS on celluloid recently it's the car that James Bond rolls in Casino Royale. And, this being an Aston, it has history.

The original, a 325bhp 4.0-litre straight-six, was introduced in 1967 and can be seen in the movie On Her Majesty's Secret Service. It's also an extension of the DB9, with only a few outward cosmetic tweaks that are aimed at improving high-performance stability and reducing kerb weight.

The DB9 may not be lacking in power and performance, but for those who want a harder edge from their Aston Martin there's the DBS. This 6.0-litre V12 petrol engine is boosted to return 512bhp, meaning that 60mph passes in just over four seconds – and the coupé keeps going all the way up to 191mph.

That's partly due to engine tweaks, but there are also carbon fibre body panels and brakes that save weight. Despite the DBS's rougher edge, the ride comfort is not compromised but the Aston feels a little more nimble than the DB9, thanks to the lower kerbweight.

There's oceans of torque from as little as 2500rpm that allows for those fast sprints, but the character of the car is very much iron fist, velvet glove. The DB9 is a wonderful tourer and cruises smoothly at motorway speeds.

There are plenty of visual cues inside the car – the Handbuilt In England inscription on the kickplates as you open the door says it all. This is a classically elegant British interior given a modern makeover. The two rear seats have been removed to make way for more luggage space so there's a definite practicality here too; a high-quality stereo, satnav from Volvo and Bluetooth connectivity provide some gadgets worthy of Bond too.

The DBS may be 'just' a harder, faster, meaner DB9, but it does evoke that old Aston machismo of the Vanquish S. It is the ultimate Aston Martin.

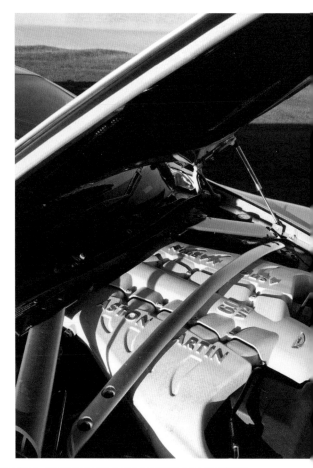

SPECIFICATION

MANUFACTURE DATE	2007-12	**ENGINE**	6.0-litre V12 petrol engine
WIDTH	1,905 mm	**TRANSMISSION**	Six-speed manual (optional 6-Speed Automatic)
HEIGHT	1,280 mm	**0-62 MPH**	4.3 seconds
LENGTH	4,722 mm	**POWER OUTPUT**	512 / bhp
MAXIMUM TORQUE	569 / nm	**BRAKES**	Front: 398 mm ventilated and drilled brakes with 6-piston alloy monobloc calipers. Rear: 360 mm ventilated and drilled brakes with 4-piston alloy monobloc calipers
MAXIMUM SPEED	191 mph	**SUSPENSION**	Adjustable double wishbone adaptive suspension

PORSCHE 911
TURBO S

One of a number of Porsche 911 derivatives that are among the fastest cars in the world, the 911 Turbo S 997 is powered by a 3.8-litre twin-turbocharged petrol engine capable of outputting 493bhp and 650Nm of torque.

The updated engine benefits from high-pressure direct fuel injection and variable turbine geometry which combines the effects of a low-rpm boost and quick responses of a small turbocharger with the high-rev power of a larger turbocharger – that flexibility provides acceleration over a wide torque band, meaning a 60mph sprint takes 3.7 seconds (3.6 with the PDK) and the top speed is of 193mph.

There are indications that the 911 Turbo is even quicker, with a 60mph time of 3.2 seconds with the semi-automatic Tiptronic transmission and a top speed of 200mph both clocked.

The 911 Turbo S gets a six-speed manual or the seven-speed PDK dual-clutch gearbox that makes the most of the hefty whack of full torque, available from just 2,100rpm. Even better there's also Porsche's own torque-vectoring system that combines a mechanical limited-slip differential, ABS and stability systems aid cornering and control.

This being a 911, styling tweaks are subtle and constrained to a slightly wider front air intake, LED indicators, daytime running lights and tail lamps, low-drag door mirrors and larger tailpipes. The PDK gets paddle-shifters mounted behind the steering wheel, instead of the disliked buttons from early PDK models.

Additional advances have been made in weight – the 911 997 Turbo weighs less than its predecessor – by 50kg. Along with the torque vectoring system, the new Porsche supercar smoothes out some of the more unpredictable kinds of the previous model and firms up handling.

Perhaps the most complete all-round car of the 911 range, at least until its replacement 991, the 997 Turbo is at once a grand tourer, supercar and everyday coupé.

SPECIFICATION

MANUFACTURE DATE	2005-11	**ENGINE**	3.8-litre twin-turbocharged petrol
WIDTH	1,855 mm	**TRANSMISSION**	Seven-speed PDK dual-clutch gearbox
HEIGHT	1,270 mm	**0-62 MPH**	3.7 seconds
LENGTH	4,245 mm	**POWER OUTPUT**	493 / bhp
MAXIMUM TORQUE	650 / nm	**BRAKES**	330 mm cross-drilled discs
MAXIMUM SPEED	193 mph	**SUSPENSION**	Wishbone with Porsche Active Suspension Management

NISSAN
GT-R
SKYLINE

Nissan has had an on-off relationship with supercars over the years, from the first Skyline back in 1969 through to the 1990 model that defined Japanese sports cars for a generation.

F ast forward 15 years and the new GT-R appeared – a 911-baiting sports coupe with plenty of performance and a low price tag. Any questions regarding Nissan's claims for the GT-R to be classed a supercar are surely dispelled by the performance figures: a huge 534bhp from a thundering 3.8-litre twin-turbo V6 go to all four wheels via a a six-speed twin-clutch gearbox and raft of active driving aids.

Astonishingly, it reaches 60mph in just 3.0 seconds, courtesy of the huge reserves of power and torque – and electronic trickery able to transmit. A launch control also aids these super-fast starts and steering-wheel mounted paddles mean that changing gear is seamless. The stability system can be configured to suit road and track driving.

The GT-R's external styling isn't subtle. It's big, chunky and aggressive but the car's apparent unwieldiness belies a stiff chassis that makes it extremely nimble when manoeuvring.

SPECIFICATION

MANUFACTURE DATE	2007	ENGINE	3.8-litre twin-turbo V6
WIDTH	1,895 mm	TRANSMISSION	Six-speed automatic dual clutch
HEIGHT	1,369 mm	0-62 MPH	3.0 seconds
LENGTH	4,656 mm	POWER OUTPUT	550 / bhp
MAXIMUM TORQUE	632 / nm	BRAKES	Brembo 6-piston aluminium monoblock calipers and 380mm drilled floating discs at front. 4-piston aluminium monoblock calipers with 380mm drilled floating discs at rear
MAXIMUM SPEED	193 mph	SUSPENSION	Bilstein damptronic fully adjustable suspension

With all of that power and torque on tap – 632Nm in the latter instance – the GT-R has excellent brakes with very little fade and awesome stopping power.

The dashboard has a vast array of instrumentation providing data on performance such as steering input degrees and cornering G-forces – but there's plenty of pleasant trim inside and arguably room for four and a good boot at 315 litres.

Just in case there are any doubts about the usability of the Nissan coupé, there's also cruise control, a good stereo system, and electrically adjustable and heated leather-trimmed seats as standard.

Still, this is a car built for performance first and foremost, with an engine that defies logic with the oceans of power and torque it can develop. With acceleration and out-and-out speed of 193mph the GT-R shames many more expensive supercars and dispels any lingering badge snobbery with its undeniable ferocious turn of pace.

TVR
TUSCAN

Few of the fastest cars are dedicated convertibles, but in the case of the TVR Tuscan, the drop-top came first and remains the essential model.

TVR's blend of raw performance, bold styling and relative affordability make it an attractive car for drivers seeking a lot of thrills for not a lot of cash. However, the TVR range does have a deserved reputation for being hardcore, not to mention being thought of as temperamental.

For raw performance the Tuscan is right up there with Porsche, Aston Martin, Ferrari and Lamborghini. The 4.0-litre S model has 400bhp, meaning a top speed of 195mph and 60mph sprint in 3.8 seconds. The all-aluminum inline Speed Six engine transmits power through a five-speed twin-plate gearbox.

For the relatively low asking price that buys all that power and performance there are obvious economies elsewhere. There's a removable roof and rear window that stows across the top of the large boot as standard, but air con was an option when the Tuscan was on sale.

There is a surprisingly big trunk, however, and in the cabin the driver is swaddled in smart leather trim that contrasts with the bare aluminium switchgear. Information is conveyed via dials and lights directly in the driver's eyeline.

The Tuscan benefited from a lot of work that went into the car's soundtrack, with the result that the car's engine unleashes an unholy roar when the throttle is opened up. Those acoustics do not misrepresent the car's abilities; at 1100kg the car is one of the lightest in the sports-car segment when compared to mainstream rivals such as Ferrari, Lamborghini and Porsche.

Without much in the way of electronic aids, the TVR Tuscan is a car that demands respect from drivers. Ferocious brakes and the relatively light kerbweight mean that the Tuscan stops as quickly as it accelerates. Added safety equipment includes integral roll over bars if the car turns over.

SPECIFICATION

MANUFACTURE DATE	1999 -2006	**ENGINE**	3996 cc six cylinders
WIDTH	1,810 mm	**TRANSMISSION**	Six speed sequential gearbox
HEIGHT	1,200 mm	**0-62 MPH**	3.8 seconds
LENGTH	4,235 mm	**POWER OUTPUT**	390 / bhp
MAXIMUM TORQUE	420 / nm	**BRAKES**	322mm ventilated discs with four-piston calipers at front; single-piston sliding caliper on 298mm discs at rear
MAXIMUM SPEED	195 mph	**SUSPENSION**	Anti-roll bar

LAMBORGHINI
GALLARDO
SUPERLEGGERA

Launched at the 2003 Geneva Motor Show, the Lamborghini Gallardo Superleggera is a lightweight version. Powered by a 40-cylinder 5.0-litre V10 petrol, the Superleggera outputs 522bhp at a high red line of 8000rpm and peak torque of 510Nm at 4250rpm – meaning a spring time of 3.8 seconds. Stopping distances have also been reduced, the reverse trip taking a whole metre less than the standard Gallardo.

To reduce kerbweight, the car makes significant use of carbon fibre – even in door panels, sports seats, engine cover and fixed rear wing; while glass is replaced with transparent polycarbonate for the engine cover and the rear window is made from similarly lightweight Macrolon.

The Superleggera – meaning lightweight – benefits from slightly more power over the Gallardo due to a remapped ECU. There's 9bhp more available at higher revs and torque output remains the same. Meanwhile there are new intake and exhaust manifolds and exhaust system.

Thin-spoke Skorpious alloy wheels are made from forged magnesium, while attention to saving weight even goes as far as titanium wheelnuts. The optional carbon-ceramic brakes fitted to our test car are no lighter than the standard cast iron set-up.

The Superleggera's engine note is especially obvious due to sound-deadening being stripped out of the engine bay. A manual gearbox or paddle-shifters are both available.

As a result of this nipping and tucking, the Superleggera is 100kg lighter than the Gallardo at 1420kg – even with a four-wheel drive system in place. For a car of its size and class the Gallardo is light indeed.

SPECIFICATION

MANUFACTURE DATE	2007	**ENGINE**	V10, 4961cc, 40v
WIDTH	1,900 mm	**TRANSMISSION**	e-gear six-speed paddle-shift
HEIGHT	1,165 mm	**0-62 MPH**	3.8 seconds
LENGTH	4,300 mm	**POWER OUTPUT**	522 / bhp @ 8000rpm
MAXIMUM TORQUE	510 / nm @ 4,250 rpm	**BRAKES**	Carbon-ceramic brake discs with six-piston calipers discs
MAXIMUM SPEED	196 mph	**SUSPENSION**	Aluminium double-wishbones front and rear suspension system, anti-roll bar

FERRARI
F430

A car frequently mentioned in relation to 'best car' lists, the Ferrari F430 was arguably the defining all-round supercar of its era. The mid-engine, rear-wheel drive Ferrari was available as a Berlinetta coupé Spider drop-top and went on sale in 2004 as a successor to the 360 Modena.

It has a new 4.3-litre V8 engine that outputs 483bhp and develops 465Nm of torque. At the time those figures meant a significant amount of power and torque, more than the 3.6-litre engine found in its predecessor.

The F430 gets a Formula 1-inspired gearbox so that gearshift take a mere 150 milliseconds – though a six-speed manual is also available. Also from motor sport is an electronic differential and a steering wheel-mounted switch that allows the driver to adjust the traction and stability-control systems. This 'manettino' – allows for five different driver modes - Ice, Low Grip and Sport through to Race and Expert – and adjusts gearshift times, engine management system and Skyhook electronic dampers stability control settings.

From the outside, the F430 gets an aluminium spaceframe and some genetic flourishes from the 360 and Enzo – it's 10 percent heavier than the 360 but benefits from improved better torsional stiffness for increased crash performance. With a new nose and tweaked aerodynamics, downforce is also improved to aid traction.

Ferrari claims the F430 will sprint to 60mph in four seconds and go on to a top speed of 196mph. But even with 483bhp and a mid-engine set-up, a new Ferrari is an amazingly user-friendly machine – the e-Diff stability control, direct steering and tons of downforce combine to make the F430 easy to drive compared to some rivals.

There's plenty of head, leg and elbow room inside with a sizeable glovebox and 250 litres of storage space under the bonnet, while the car's Daytona-style upholstery befits the price tag. The leather and carbon fibre steering wheel is a particularly pleasant addition.

All of this makes the Ferrari F430 an awesome track car with enough day to day usability and interior ambience to qualify as one of the most dramatic-looking daily drives.

SPECIFICATION

MANUFACTURE DATE	2004-09	**ENGINE**	4.3-litre V8 engine
WIDTH	1,923 mm	**TRANSMISSION**	Six-speed F1-style electrohydraulic manual
HEIGHT	1,214 mm	**0-62 MPH**	4.0 seconds
LENGTH	4,511 mm	**POWER OUTPUT**	483 / bhp
MAXIMUM TORQUE	465 / nm	**BRAKES**	Double unequal-length wishbone suspension set-up front and rear with anti-dive and anti-squat geometries
MAXIMUM SPEED	196 mph	**SUSPENSION**	Cast-iron Brembo disc brakes with molybdenum; four-piston calipers

AUDI
R8 V10

The Audi R8 V8 is hardly lacking in firepower, but for those seeking a little more Lamborghini in their Audi supercar there's the R8 V10. Packing the Gallardo's 5.2-litre V10 petrol engine, the R8 V10 develops 543bhp, which propels the R8 to 60mph in 3.9 seconds and tops out at almost 200mph.

There's not just power, but torque too. The engine revs to 8,700rpm so gearing is extremely flexible and acceleration formidable. The V10 Plus gets the new S tronic seven-speed auto, whose superfast gear changes make the sprint possible in just 3.5 seconds. It also gets a lowered and stiffened fixed-rate sports suspension for even sharper handling, while ceramic brakes – standard on the V10 Plus – give stopping ability that is almost brake-fade free.

Handling on the standard model is designed to be comfortable, with Comfort Magnetic-fluid damping as standard smoothing out the ride, but handling is tight, flexible and communicative due to rear-wheel drive with the back-up of torque distribution to all four wheels should it be required, courtesy of the quattro four-wheel-drive system.

Coupe and soft-top Spyder models are both available, with little drop-off in drivability in the convertible.

All models come with LED daytime running lights and LED rear indicators but the V10 gets special Y-design 19-inch alloy wheels and more pronounced side-blades. There's also satnav, Audi Music Interface with integrated Bluetooth, heated seats and all-LED lights.

In the supercar stakes, the addition of extra power and torque means the R8 V10 faces off against the likes of the Porsche 911 and Aston Martin Vantage, but the likes of the Ferrari 458 Italia and stablemate Lamborghini Gallardo are also on the radar of the Audi supercar.

SPECIFICATION

MANUFACTURE DATE	2008	**ENGINE**	5.2-litre V10 petrol
WIDTH	2,029 mm	**TRANSMISSION**	Seven-speed auto S tronic
HEIGHT	1,252 mm	**0-62 MPH**	3.9 seconds
LENGTH	4,431 mm	**POWER OUTPUT**	543 / bhp
MAXIMUM TORQUE	530 / nm	**BRAKES**	Wave brake discs, internally ventilated, 8-piston brake calipers at front; 4-piston at rear
MAXIMUM SPEED	196 mph	**SUSPENSION**	Sports suspension with dynamically tuned spring and damper combination

BMW
ALPINA B5 S

Based on the BMW M5, the ALPINA B5 S is one of the fastest BMWs in the manufacturer's history; capable of phenomenal speed for a donor car more apt for motorway and Autobahn cruising.

Where BMW has traditionally eschewed forced induction and automatic gearboxes, the B5 S makes use of both – meaning 197mph is possible in this large executive four-door sedan, putting it among the fastest of its kind in the world. To put that into perspective, from a standing start the Alpina B5 S can theoretically beat the Aston Martin DBS to a kilometre.

The S version is powered by the BMW 4.4-litre supercharged V8 but this one puts out 530bhp through a six-speed automatic gearbox controlled via two buttons on the back of the steering wheel.

Despite the car's weight, the Alpina S has a frightening turn of pace courtesy of a staggering 725Nm of torque that's noticeable throughout the rev range. A limited-slip differential keeps the rear wheels in check.

20-inch alloy wheels also ensure the Alpina is able to transmit all that power, but there's also help from the suspension, BMW's Electronic Damper Control and the ability to change suspension settings depending on requirements. Choose the Sport button and throttle responses sharpen up significantly, revealing the B5 S's trackday potential.

SPECIFICATION

MANUFACTURE DATE	2005	**ENGINE**	V8, 4398cc, supercharged biturbo
WIDTH	1,860 mm	**TRANSMISSION**	Eight-speed auto, rear-wheel drive
HEIGHT	1,464 mm	**0-62 MPH**	4.6 seconds
LENGTH	4,899 mm	**POWER OUTPUT**	523 bhp @ 5500 rpm
MAXIMUM TORQUE	535 lb ft @ 4750 rpm	**BRAKES**	374mm and 370mm front to rear with automatic brake drying
MAXIMUM SPEED	197 mph	**SUSPENSION**	Alpina Sport Suspension

However, Comfort and Normal settings make the B5 S a potential daily drive too – preferring an element of refinement to the manic M5. The B5 S provides an alternative to the M5 for drivers seeking a more usable car, with a more pliant ride than the BMW donor car.

The Alpina arguably takes the edge off the M5, but it still packs a phenomenal amount of power; it remains a four-door family car that can manage almost 200mph.

FERRARI 612 SCAGLIETTI

The 540bhp, rear-drive Ferrari 612 Scaglietti was claimed to be the fastest four-door in the world when it went on sale. While Bentley may have had something to say about that, the official top speed is an impressive 199mph.

That's courtesy of a 532bhp 5.7-litre V12 that sent 588Nm of torque to the rear wheels and propelled the 612 to 60mph in just over four seconds. Power delivery is languid and the plentiful low-end torque is progressive all the way up to 5250rpm.

The rear-mounted gearbox shifts fluently, especially in auto mode, while driver-dialled dynamic settings mean the 612 can be driven as a luxury grand tourer or legitimately be taken onto the track. Hit Sport mode and the 612's electronic aids back off.

Transmissions include a six-speed F1 single-clutch automated manual and Ferrari's manettino – and F1-inspired dial on the steering wheel that allows the driver to select one of five different driving modes – was added to later models.

Meanwhile speed-sensitive steering that's light at high speeds and heavier around town to boost everyday drivability, despite the car's whopping 4902mm length.

The 612's cabin is roomy, the dashboard a winning mix of analogue and digital dials and there is a reminder of Ferrari heritage in a plaque listing Ferrari's five recent F1 world constructor championship titles.

The four seats are firm, supportive and electrically adjustable and do genuinely allow for four passengers. The 612 may defy easy categorization, but with an equipment list that includes the likes of xenon headlights, an adaptive suspension system, a power-closing boot, parking sensors, navigation system and Bose audio system with Bluetooth wireless connectivity and a 15GB music server the car is best thought of as a performance grand tourer.

The 612 Scaglietti's motorsport underpinnings ensure that the Ferrari can match similar grand tourers for performance, yet the fundamentally unhurried nature of the car also ensures the 612 is a genuine potential daily drive.

SPECIFICATION

MANUFACTURE DATE	2004-11	ENGINE	5.7 L Tipo F133F V12
WIDTH	1,956 mm	TRANSMISSION	Six-speed manual or Six-speed F1A semi-auto
HEIGHT	1,344 mm	0-62 MPH	4.3 seconds
LENGTH	4,902 mm	POWER OUTPUT	532 / bhp
MAXIMUM TORQUE	588 / nm	BRAKES	8-piston calipers and 380mm ceramic discs front; 4-piston calipers and 380mm ceramic discs rear
MAXIMUM SPEED	199 mph	SUSPENSION	Double-wishbone suspension's adaptive damping

BENTLEY CONTINENTAL
FLYING SILVER SPUR

Bentley's famously quick Speed models first appeared in 1923, and the 600bhp Bentley Continental Flying Spur Speed is inspired by this legacy. It's the fastest four-door Bentley, promising unparalleled levels of agility and driver engagement, whilst offering the uncompromising drive performance and comfort that Bentley is known for.

With the 600bhp 6.0-litre W12 engine from the Continental GT Speed coupé, the four-door Bentley Flying Spur Speed is a 2.5-tonne giant that's also frighteningly quick. The Flying SpurSpeed is capable of hitting 60mph in 4.5 seconds and goes on to a top speed of 200mph through the uprated W12's engine management system. Bentley raised power output and torque meaning that 750Nm was available from just 1,750rpm.

To exploit this massive power and torque, the spring/damper settings and anti-roll bars were specially uprated, as was a retuned speed-sensitive steering system. A revised Bosch stability control system allowed for more progressive, subtle intervention – a Dynamic Mode allowed increased wheel slip at higher speeds.

With a harder edge and sportier feel, it also offers tauter handling and nimbler steering response than its sister model. The Flying Spur Speed benefits from a redesigned suspension, a lowered ride height and retuned steering for improved agility and body control. Bentley claimed that with its revised ESP system and suspension the Continental Flying Spur Speed was capable of stopping from 60mph in 33 metres and handling over 0.95 g-forces of lateral acceleration.

There are some subtle design cues that signal the Bentley Flying Spur Speed's identity, including a dark tinted front grille and lower air intakes, wider rifled exhaust pipes, Speed treadplates on all four door sills, a three-spoke sport leather steering wheel, drilled alloy pedals and a knurled chrome and hide gear lever.

There is also a classical English quality to the interior – the car boasts leather, wood, or metal on every surface touched by the occupant, while options include fine furniture-quality service trays with vanity mirrors.

SPECIFICATION

MANUFACTURE DATE	2009-2013	**ENGINE**	6.0 L W12 twin-turbo
WIDTH	1,915 mm	**TRANSMISSION**	Six-speed ZF 6HP26A tiptronic auto
HEIGHT	1,478 mm	**0-62 MPH**	4.5 seconds
LENGTH	5,306 mm	**POWER OUTPUT**	600 / bhp
MAXIMUM TORQUE	750 / nm	**BRAKES** Ceramic disc brakes, and an upgraded Bosch ESP 8.1 Electronic Stability Programme	
MAXIMUM SPEED	200 mph	**SUSPENSION** Four-link suspension at front; trapezoidal multi-link system at the rear. 10mm lowered	

BENTLEY CONTINENTAL GT

The Bentley Continental GT is a stunning coupé that blends classic Bentley DNA with contemporary design and modern technology – offering a combination of supercar performance and handcrafted luxury.

The Continental GT is perhaps the ultimate Grand Tourer, boasting then-revolutionary suspension when the coupe hit the roads in 2003, including Intelligent Continuous Damping Control that constantly monitors the car's attitude and poise, adjusting the suspension hundreds of times a second to alter ride stiffness depending on circumstances and road quality.

The Continental GT was all-wheel drive, with the car's vast amounts of power and torque distributed through all four wheels, with a 40:60 split power ratio for added security in difficult conditions and improved cornering – an uprated Electronic Stability Control was also added.

The 12-cylinder 6.0-litre W12 engine was the most compact 12-cylinder engine in the world at the time and capable of running on petrol, bioethanol or a combination of the two.

With its power output raised to 567bhp and torque up to 700Nm through an eight-speed Quickshift transmission, the Conti GT can go from a standstill to 60mph in just 4.4 seconds and reach a top speed of 200mph.

All Bentley models are famously handmade at the manufacturer's Crewe factory. Over 80 per cent of the entire cabin is trimmed with soft-touch leather, while the GT has a full range of wood veneers, cool-touch metals and deep-pile carpets.

SPECIFICATION

MANUFACTURE DATE	2003	**ENGINE**	6-litre W12 twin-turbocharged Flexfuel
WIDTH	2,227 mm	**TRANSMISSION**	Eight-speed Quickshift
HEIGHT	1, 404 mm	**0-62 MPH**	4.4 seconds
LENGTH	4,806 mm	**POWER OUTPUT**	567 / bhp
MAXIMUM TORQUE	700 / nm	**BRAKES**	Vented front and rear disc brakes
MAXIMUM SPEED	200 mph	**SUSPENSION**	Air springs with Continuous Damping Control (CDC)

ASCARI
KZ1

British company Ascari produced its
first supercar, the Ecosse, in 1998
but it was the KZ1 in 2003 that made
the company's name.

U sing a 500bhp 5.0-litre V8 sourced from
BMW, mid-mounted and mated to a
six-speed manual gearbox, it propelled
the KZ1 to 200mph and ensured a 60mph sprint
of 3.7 seconds and 100mph in eight.

With a power-to-weight ratio of 370bhp per tonne
and torque of 550Nm at 4500rpm, the KZ also
benefited from a lightweight carbon fibre design
meaning a kerbweight of 1300kg KZ1.

The Ascari KZ1's engine was mounted
longitudinally behind the driver, while the
six-speed Cima gearbox is also seen in
Pagani and Koenigsegg models.

The Ascari boasted a carbon body on a carbon honeycomb monocoque chassis and a double wishbone suspension and AP Racing brakes. This meant the KZ1 was a superb handling car that was available with a bespoke suspension set-up and had input from Lotus Engineering.

The KZ1's fully adjustable suspension was softly sprung and damping ensured first-class body control; bespoke suspension could be specified by clients depending on requirements and preference. As a comfortable and refined Autobahn model and a track-day hero the KZ1 delivered in spades; however only 50 were ever produced.

The Ascari KZ1 retains one of the fastest times ever around the Top Gear test track.

SPECIFICATION

MANUFACTURE DATE	2003-2010	**ENGINE**	V8, 4941cc
WIDTH	2,852 mm	**TRANSMISSION**	Eight-speed Quickshift
HEIGHT	1,138 mm	**0-62 MPH**	3.6 seconds
LENGTH	4,300 mm	**POWER OUTPUT**	500 / bhp @ 7,000rpm
MAXIMUM TORQUE	368lb ft @ 4,800 rpm	**BRAKES**	Cross-drilled and vented discs w/AP Racing 6-piston calipers at front cross-drilled and vented discs w/AP Racing 4-piston calipers
MAXIMUM SPEED	200 mph	**SUSPENSION**	Double-wishbones with coil-over dampers, Anti-Roll Bar at front and rear

FAST CARS
200-210
MPH

FERRARI
F40

When the Ferrari F40 was launched in 1984 it was the fastest supercar in the world, topping out at 201mph.

Designed to celebrate the 40th anniversary of Ferrari car production, hence the F40 name, the supercar was a replacement for the popular 288 GTO but soon became one of the most iconic Ferrari cars of all time.

The Ferrari F40 is a particularly stripped-back car with a focus on lightweight architecture – carbon fibre and aluminium are used unsparingly throughout – and its aerodynamic design makes use of the 2.9-litre V8 engine developing 471bhp.

At 4500rpm, the Ferrari F40 delivers 577Nm of torque and everything about the drive train was upgraded from the Ferrari 288 GTO it replaced, including improvements to its displacement, compression ratio and even turbochargers.

Everything about the F40 is aimed at delivering a focused driving experience and the car has been shorn of any extras that do not contribute to the on-road dynamics.

Renowned for providing a visceral driving thrill like no other, the Ferrari F40 uses a mid-engine, rear-wheel drive setup and, while the 0-62mph sprint time is an impressive 3.7 seconds, it is the manner of the delivery that makes this one of the best supercars ever made.

SPECIFICATION

MANUFACTURE DATE	1987-1992	**ENGINE**	2.9-litre V8 petrol
WIDTH	1,980 mm	**TRANSMISSION**	Five-speed manual
HEIGHT	1, 130 mm	**0-62 MPH**	3.7 seconds
LENGTH	4,430 mm	**POWER OUTPUT**	471 / bhp
MAXIMUM TORQUE	557 / nm	**BRAKES**	13.0-in. vented discs/ 13.0-in. vented discs
MAXIMUM SPEED	201 mph	**SUSPENSION**	Wishbones with coil springs over adjustable Koni shock absorbers. Front and rear anti-roll bars. Electronically adjustable suspension as an option

Driving the F40 is an incredible experience; the suspension is stiff and steering responsive at higher speeds and the feeling of speed is amplified by the feel of every bump in the road. Famed for its ability to catch out the inexperienced driver once it is up to speed, the Ferrari F40 is a brute of a supercar.

For many, the outrageous supercar looks, including that huge rear spoiler and road-hugging stance and ferocious driving performance, put the Ferrari F40 at the top of the pile when it comes to supercars.

Ferrari went on to build over 1,300 F40s, all painted red, and as a result it is not the rarest supercar the brand has produced. However, it was the last commissioned by Enzo Ferrari and probably the best-loved model to come from the Ferrari stable.

LAMBORGHINI GALLARDO LP560-4

The Lamborghini Gallardo LP560-4 is an improved version of the brand's most recognisable car and delivers awe-inspiring performance and power.

Before its 2008 launch, the Gallardo name already had a reputation for fearsome performance where power outweighed refinement for a full-blooded driving experience.

All sharp lines and aggressive style, the Gallardo design has been unchanged, on the surface at least, for many years. However, the latest iteration to use the Gallardo name does boast some subtle tweaks including a more aerodynamic body and weight loss of around 20kg over the previous generation.

The Lamborghini Gallardo LP560-4 added more power to the Gallardo courtesy of a 5.2-litre V10 engine that delivers 552bhp. This provides a top speed of 202mph and a 0-62mph sprint time of 3.7 seconds.

Power goes to all four wheels and with 398lb of torque at 6500rpm this is necessary to distribute the sheer power of the V10 powerplant.

The Lamborghini has a reputation as a car that is brash and wild but the LP560-4 does offer subtle upgrades to reduce the chance of losing control in corners. This includes a revamped suspension to give the car more stability in corners and smoother suspension.

However, the throaty roar of the V10 engine remains and continues to be the main aspect drivers of this car take away from the experience. More refined than ever, it rises to a crescendo as the car moves through the gears ensuring the driver makes no mistake about the level of power on offer.

Inside the Lamborghini Gallardo LP560-4 the car benefits from the quality delivered by parent group Volkswagen. Meanwhile, an 18 per cent cut in CO_2 emissions and a pedestrian-friendly front end point to a more responsible, practical supercar.

While that may be the case the new refined Lamborghini Gallardo LP560-4 is still a superb supercar in every sense. Its razor-sharp lines are sure to stir something within every car fan and the roar of the engine is still one of the most thrilling sounds on the road today.

SPECIFICATION

MANUFACTURE DATE	2008	**ENGINE**	5.2-litre V10 petrol
WIDTH	1,900 mm	**TRANSMISSION** Six-speed manual or six-speed E-gear	
HEIGHT	1, 165 mm	**0-62 MPH**	3.7 seconds
LENGTH	4,386 mm	**POWER OUTPUT**	542 / bhp
MAXIMUM TORQUE	540 / nm	**BRAKES**	365 x 34 mm (14.4- x 1.33-inch) steel ventilated rotors (front) and 356 x 32 mm (14.01- x 1.25-inch) ventilated rotors (back).
MAXIMUM SPEED	202 mph	**SUSPENSION**	Double-wishbone construction on the front and rear

FERRARI
575M

The Ferrari 575M Maranello F1 is a supercar that breaks the mould when it comes to Ferrari racers.

Launched in the early 2000s as a successor to the Ferrari 550 the 575M is famed for matching speed with driveability. This is a car that provides all the pace of a top-level supercar but is less likely to leave the inexperienced driver in the ditch.

The Ferrari 575M is perhaps most notable for the introduction of the F1-style paddle shifter. The six-speed semi-automatic gearbox delivers smoother shifting as the car accelerates to deliver an even better driving experience.

The engine is a V12 monster delivering 515bhp and a Sport mode is available to increase the speed of upshifts and downshifts. The Sport mode also adapts the shock-absorbers for a greater body control at higher speeds.

The engine includes an increase in bore by a single millimetre to boost engine displacement and improves the compression ratio to cope with the addition of the new F1 gearbox. The automatic transmission is by far the most popular but a six-speed manual is also available on the Ferrari 575M.

All this power can send the car over 200mph with ease and the Ferrari 575M is capable of a 0-62mph sprint time of 4.2 seconds. A launch control system ensures the car is quick off the line and gives the 575M a sense of urgency when taking off.

The Ferrari 575M is one of the more poised supercars. Excellent 50-50 weight distribution over the axles means drivers will not be caught out by understeer even at higher speeds.

The two-seat supercar is also available with a GTC handling package which was added a couple of years after its launch and adds a composite ceramic Brembo brake system and suspension tuned for track-based performance.

The Ferrari 575M also comes with a luxurious interior courtesy of Carrozzeria Scaglietti and includes two eight-way adjustable seats and a range of customization options covering everything from colours to cabin equipment.

SPECIFICATION

MANUFACTURE DATE	2002-2006	**ENGINE**	5.7-litre 48v V12
WIDTH	1,935mm	**TRANSMISSION**Six-speed semi-auto, rear-wheel drive	
HEIGHT	1,277 mm	**0-62 MPH**	4.2 seconds
LENGTH	4,550 mm	**POWER OUTPUT**	515 / bhp
MAXIMUM TORQUE	589 / nm	**BRAKES**	Cross Drilled and Vented Discs w/ABS
MAXIMUM SPEED	202 mph	**SUSPENSION**	Double-wishbones with coil Springs plus anti-roll bar

FERRARI F50

How do you follow a car like the Ferrari F40? For the Italian car maker, the only option was to add more power and a more raw driving experience.

E nter the Ferrari F50, a distinctive supercar that delivers racing performance and an ostentatious design that guarantees driving one will attract plenty of attention.

Described by Ferrari as the closest thing to a road-going F1 car, the F50 is an incredible machine that was limited to just over 300 units, creating a rarity and high price that puts it out of reach of most supercar fans.

While the F40 was a highly stylised design, the F50 is heavily influenced by F1 cars with a road-hugging stance, huge rear spoiler and sweeping curves.

The influences from the peak of motorsport include a carbon fibre monocoque that provides enough integrity to cosset the driver in the event of an accident. In the case of the F50, Ferrari knew it would need to be secure enough for road use.

On the road, the F50 has a reputation for being an unruly powerhouse. The reputation is fitting; the Ferrari F50 packs in 520bhp from the V12 engine, which itself was inspired by the brand's F1 cars of the 1990s.

If that was not enough, the F50 does not come with power assistance for the brakes and steering giving the car a more involved – and harder to control – drive.

The Ferrari F50 is quicker than the F40 it replaced. The F1-style improvements mean a top speed of 207mph is possible and the 0-62mph sprint time is just 3.7 seconds.

Its 4.7-litre V12 engine churns out an incredible 750bhp and 471Nm of torque at 6500rpm and this power, along with a raw driving experience, is often levelled as a criticism of the brash F50.

However, there is no doubt the car delivers a unique driving experience and the addition of a removable hard top means the sound of the V12 engine can be enjoyed in the open air.

The Ferrari F50 was first introduced in 1995, the brand's 50th anniversary, and production lasted just two years.

SPECIFICATION

MANUFACTURE DATE	1995 -1997	ENGINE	4.7-litre V12
WIDTH	1,986 mm	TRANSMISSION	Six-speed manual, limited slip differential
HEIGHT	1,120 mm	0-62 MPH	3.7 seconds
LENGTH	4,480 mm	POWER OUTPUT	750 / bhp
MAXIMUM TORQUE	471 / nm	BRAKES	Brembo cross-drilled & ventilated cast iron discs, 4 piston aluminium Brembo calipers. No ABS.
MAXIMUM SPEED	207 mph	SUSPENSION	Rose-jointed unequal-length wishbones. Front and rear anti-roll bars

PORSCHE 911
GT2

The Porsche 911 inspires fierce loyalty from its supporters and the Porsche 911 GT2 has a special place in petrolhead hearts because it was the first car to bear the 911 name to reach 200mph.

The Porsche 911 GT2 can reach 204mph in total and the first 62mph of that can be reached in just 3.6 seconds.

What makes the Porsche 922 GT2 so fast compared to the standard 911 Turbo is the decision to do away with the all-wheel drive system and instead use rear-wheel drive.

This has the benefit of reducing enough weight to reach 200mph with ease. The engine is a 3.6-litre flat-six developing 530bhp and 680Nm of torque at 4500rpm. There are no doubts the Porsche 911 is quick and the interior design of the car lends itself to this perception of speed.

While the 911 GT2 does come with the usual radio and air conditioning combination, the interior is as stripped-back as possible. This means two sports seats surrounded by a steel roll cage in the rear. While luggage space is almost non-existent, this is a car that is not intended as a practical runaround.

The 911 GT2 is lower and lighter than the Turbo version of the 911 and features stiffened suspension to improve handling.

With that bulky rear end providing all the power and semi-slick tyres not usually associated with providing grip, the Porsche 911 does leave you thinking the back end will flick out at corners.

The Porsche 911 GT2 is not for the faint-hearted and the noise of the engine coming from behind reminds drivers of the challenge that faces them from the rear-wheel drive setup.

However, automatic suspension will help to allay any fears in the 911 GT2 and leave you enjoying the thrill of the poised, powerful and lightweight Porsche.

The Porsche 911 range has been diluted with an almost endless list of special editions and variations on the iconic shape. The Porsche 911 GT2 is something completely different and is a worthy addition to the ranks of genuine supercars.

SPECIFICATION

MANUFACTURE DATE	2008	**ENGINE**	3.6-litre flat-six petrol
WIDTH	1,852 mm	**TRANSMISSION**	Six-speed manual
HEIGHT	1,303 mm	**0-62 MPH**	3.6 seconds
LENGTH	4,491 mm	**POWER OUTPUT**	530 / bhp
MAXIMUM TORQUE	680 / nm	**BRAKES**	Porsche Ceramic Composite Brakes
MAXIMUM SPEED	204 mph	**SUSPENSION**	Electronically controlled PASM Porsche Active Suspension Management. (PASM)

CORVETTE
ZR1

The ZR1 is not only the fastest Corvette
ever built but it is also the only model that
can challenge the world's best supercars
when it comes to speed.

The ZR1 is based on the Corvette C6 but
adds more performance and technology to
create the most powerful and advanced car
in the Corvette range.

The road-ready racer tops out at 205mph and can move from standing to 62mph in just 3.4 seconds. Power is delivered by a 6.2-litre V8 engine producing 638bhp and 819Nm of torque at 4000rpm, helped along by a four-lobe supercharger as opposed to the three-lobe versions used in other Corvette cars.

Chevrolet makes extensive use of carbon fibre throughout the Corvette ZR1 including the hood and roof. Meanwhile, a clear window exposes the impressive engine intercooler daubed with the ZR1 name.

The Corvette delivers supreme handling on both road and track and in the latter situation Sport mode can be switched on and traction systems can be toned down at the push of a button.

The introduction of a Magnetic Selective Ride Control (MSRC) suspension system similar to those used on top Ferrari cars, automatically adjusts suspension settings based on weather and road conditions and the car dips into the garage of another supercar, the Bugatti Veyron, for its 15.5-inch Brembo carbon-ceramic brakes.

SPECIFICATION

MANUFACTURE DATE	2009	**ENGINE**	6.2-litre / V8
WIDTH	1,852 mm	**TRANSMISSION**	Six-speed manual Tremec TR-6060
HEIGHT	1,240 mm	**0-62 MPH**	3.4 seconds
LENGTH	4,480 mm	**POWER OUTPUT**	638 / bhp
MAXIMUM TORQUE	819 / nm	**BRAKES**	Carbon Ceramic Brakes. At front Brembo 6-piston calipers, at rear 4-piston calipers
MAXIMUM SPEED	205 mph	**SUSPENSION**	Double-wishbones with Magnetic Selective Ride Control

Launch and traction control were added in later models and the car is much more manageable at higher speeds as a result. The system will control the amount of power to the wheels if the car is struggling for grip and make life significantly easier for the driver.

While it is being driven, an advanced dual-mode performance exhaust system creates plenty of noise – there is nothing quite like the sound of a Corvette in full flow and clever cabin acoustics allow the sound of the ZR1 to be enjoyed as it is driven.

Corvette ZR1 drivers also get leather-clad bucket seats, climate control and a seven-speaker sound system among other equipment in the luxurious supercar.

FERRARI
599 GTB

The Ferrari 599 GTB is a supercar that matches F1-style technology with a typically emotive design that represents the car maker's signature.

The two-seat Ferrari 599 GTB was introduced in 2007 as a replacement for the 575 and delivers even more performance than its predecessor.

Often referred to as the Fiorano after the Ferrari race track on which its ride and handling were honed, the 599 GTB has a reputation as one of the best-loved Ferrari gran turismo models.

Capable of reaching 205mph, it uses a 6.0-litre V12 engine producing 661 bhp and owners get a choice of six-speed manual gearbox or a six-speed 'F1 Superfast' option.

The F1 Superfast gearbox is lifted from the brand's successful F1 cars and delivers ultra-fast gear changes via steering wheel paddles. Ferrari estimates gear changes take just 100ms in performance situations.

Despite being the most powerful Ferrari ever sold when it arrived, the Ferrari 599 GTB is notable for its controlled, comfortable ride as a result of F1-inspired technology.

Ferrari's Magneride suspension adapts the car to suit driving conditions and the F1-trac control system is designed to read handling data and change the brakes and suspension accordingly. This allows the car to feel comfortable in straight lines but sharp around corners.

As a result the rear-wheel drive supercar is perfect for taking onto a track and the sheer power and noise coming from the engine bay will deliver pure driving pleasure.

Ferrari has developed the exhaust and cabin to improve the quality of the sound being delivered into the cabin via a tube feeding the intake sound towards the driver and passenger The Ferrari 599 GTB was eventually replaced by the Ferrari F12 Berlinetta but many will class this as one of the most technically advanced supercars to ever grace the road.

An optional package called the HGTE package is also available for the 599 GTB which improves handling by delivering stiffened springs, a rear anti-roll bar and tweaks to the Magneride system for a more track-based driving feel.

SPECIFICATION

MANUFACTURE DATE	2007	**ENGINE**	6.0-litre / V12
WIDTH	1,962 mm	**TRANSMISSION**	Six-speed manual or F1 Superfast gearbox with steering-mounted paddles
HEIGHT	1,336 mm	**0-62 MPH**	3.3 seconds
LENGTH	4,665 mm	**POWER OUTPUT**	661 / bhp
MAXIMUM TORQUE	620 / nm	**BRAKES**	13.9 x 1.3 in (front) and 12.9 x 1.1 in (rear)carbon ceramic brakes
MAXIMUM SPEED	205 mph	**SUSPENSION**	Magneride suspension capable of adapting to road conditions. F1-Trac manages data and adjusts settings accordingly

MASERATI
MC12

The Maserati MC12 is a two-seat supercar with more than a little in common with the Ferrari Enzo. In fact, the MC12 is actually based on an Enzo platform but comes with a revamped design.

It took an extensive makeover for the Maserati MC12 to emerge in its current guise and nearly all parts have been replaced. As a result the MC12 feels like a unique car – and a limited production run of just 50 mean it is also an incredibly rare car.

To transform the Enzo, Maserati extended the wheelbase and stretched out the car for better aerodynamics including the addition of a rear spoiler to boost down-force at higher speeds.

The two-door supercar has a mid-rear layout using a 6.0-litre V12 engine taken from the Ferrari Enzo. The engine delivers 600bhp at 7200rpm and 655Nm at 5500rpm and helps to propel the car to a top speed of 205mph.

Weight distribution is 41 per cent front and 59 per cent rear while the use of carbon fibre and other alloys have kept weight to a minimum on the MC12.

The sequential six-speed gearbox is operated by paddles and the car roars through the lower gears to deliver supreme acceleration – it can reach 62mph in just 3.8 seconds from standing.

The size and power of the Maserati MC12 means it is one of the more challenging cars to drive even with traction control turned on. The lack of rear window can hinder visibility as well – but there is the option of removing the roof to turn it into a convertible.

Originally designed for the track, the Maserati MC12 has had to undergo some tweaks to ensure it can be used on the road. The cabin is obviously influenced by its racing heritage with a flat-topped steering wheel, carbon fibre and leather surfaces and sports seats – but the cabin does lack some comforts such as a radio or sound system.

The Maserati MC12 is essentially a track car that has undergone some small tweaks to allow it to be road legal and all 50 editions are available in a single colour choice; blue and white.

SPECIFICATION

MANUFACTURE DATE	2004	ENGINE	6.0-litre / V12
WIDTH	2,100 mm	TRANSMISSION	Six-speed Maserati Cambiocorsa
HEIGHT	1,205 mm	0-62 MPH	3.7 seconds
LENGTH	5,143 mm	POWER OUTPUT	600 / bhp
MAXIMUM TORQUE	655 / nm	BRAKES	Brembo front brakes with six-piston calipers and the rear brakes with four-piston calipers
MAXIMUM SPEED	205 mph	SUSPENSION	Independent wishbone suspension with push-rod actuated dampers

FORD
GT

The Ford GT is a muscular, two-seat supercar based on the iconic GT racers of the 1960s and built in limited numbers.

Only 5000 Ford GT models were built between 2005 and 2006 as Ford took on the supercar heavyweights of Ferrari and Lamborghini.

To do this, Ford uses a 5.4-litre supercharged V8 matched to a six-speed manual gearbox. The engine outputs 530bhp at 6500rpm and 678Nm of torque at 3750rpm and delivers impressive performance statistics.

Reaching 62mph from standing takes just 3.2 seconds and in just 7.4 seconds the car can travel at 100mph. It goes on to achieve a top speed of 205mph to match many of its more illustrious rivals.

The mid-engine layout negates the need for traction control in the GT and the engine is matched to a six-speed transmission.

It would be easy to consider the Ford GT as a way of cashing in on one of Ford's most iconic models – the racing GT40s from the 1960s – but the GT is an excellent car in its own right.

Built using an aluminium space frame chassis as opposed to the carbon fibre used by rivals, the Ford GT has been designed with speed and safety in mind.

Ford has designed the GT in the spirit of its iconic American muscle cars and amount of grunt on offer testifies to the success of this theme. The Ford GT delivers tremendous amounts of power and raw pace but can still be considered an everyday supercar.

Inside the cabin the clean, clear controls and comfortable seating area are a welcome change in the supercar segment but the car does have a sting in its tail when it comes to oversteer – something that will delight those who wish to take it on to a track.

Above all else the Ford GT is a car that is to be seen in and the level of exterior detail, iconic Ford racing stripes and distinctive, box-like rear end means the Ford GT remains an extremely popular supercar.

SPECIFICATION

MANUFACTURE DATE	2005 -2006	**ENGINE**	5.4-litre supercharged V8
WIDTH	1,950 mm	**TRANSMISSION**	Ricardo-sourced six-speed manual
HEIGHT	1,130 mm	**0-62 MPH**	3.2 seconds
LENGTH	4,640 mm	**POWER OUTPUT**	530 / bhp
MAXIMUM TORQUE	678 / nm	**BRAKES** Four-piston aluminium Brembo calipers with cross-drilled and vented rotors at all four corners.	
MAXIMUM SPEED	205 mph	**SUSPENSION** Double-wishbone suspension design with unequal-length aluminium control arms, coil-over monotube shocks and stabilizer bars	

CAPARO
T1

The Caparo T1 is a British-built supercar described by designer Ben Scott-Geddes as the closest thing to a roadworthy Formula One car on sale today.

A quick glance at the two-seat racer indicates that may not be too far from the truth. The Caparo T1 hugs the road between large, curved wheel arches and boasts a rear spoiler to boost down force.

The two seats include six-point harnesses and the lightweight racer has been stripped of all superfluous equipment that could push up the weight of the car.

Before entering the car there is an adjustable twin element front and rear wing that can be replaced with road or track variations depending on where the car is being driven.

Performance statistics are particularly impressive. A curb weight of just 480kg means the Caparo T1 can make the most of its 3.5-litre naturally aspirated V8 engine.

The engine delivers 575bhp and is matched to a six-speed sequential gearbox than tops out at 10,500rpm. At 9000rpm the car produces 420Nm of torque and, as a result, the Caparo T1 can reach a top speed of 205mph.

The Caparo T1 is also one of the fastest accelerating cars in the world, reaching 62mph from standing in less than 2.5 seconds and 100mph in 4.9 seconds. This is a car that is not far off the fastest in the world and means it can justifiably make the F1 claims.

The power-to-weight ratio makes for a thrilling ride but as a track-style racer its use as a daily drive is limited. This power can really be felt through 3g of lateral acceleration and deceleration, more than three times the amount compared to most standard road cars.

Its low body design, much like that of F1 prototypes, and powerful engine means the Caparo T1 can be a challenge to drive on the road because of its low ground clearance.

Only a handful of Caparo T1 cars have been built by small British manufacturer Caparo Vehicle Technologies and it remains a niche vehicle sold in small numbers.

SPECIFICATION

MANUFACTURE DATE	2012	ENGINE	3.5-litre naturally aspirated V8 engine
WIDTH	1,990 mm	TRANSMISSION	Six-speed manual sequential gearbox
HEIGHT	1,076 mm	0-62 MPH	2.5 seconds
LENGTH	4,066 mm	POWER OUTPUT	575 / bhp
MAXIMUM TORQUE	420 / nm	BRAKES	355-millimetre (14.0 in) steel brake discs, with six-piston and four-piston calipers front and rear
MAXIMUM SPEED	205 mph	SUSPENSION	Double-wishbone design with adjustable front and rear stabilizers and five-way adjustable dampers

BMW
M5

When BMW revealed that the latest version of its sporty M5 super sedan would be sold with a V8 engine instead of the traditional V10, it raised a few eyebrows.

It represented the first time a BMW M5 had replaced an engine with one with fewer cylinders and could have been argued as toning down a range known for its immense power.

Luckily this was not the case for the 4.4-litre V8 turbocharged BMW M5 producing 552bhp – it delivers ten per cent more power than the V10 engine it replaces while still improving fuel economy by as much as 30 per cent.

The extra performance translates into a top speed of 205mph but this has been limited on production versions to just 155mph.

Despite weighing nearly 2,000kg the BMW M5 is no slouch. It can accelerate from 0-62mph in 3.7 seconds and because of the use of turbocharging it offers more low-end torque than the V10 version.

The BMW M5 is one of the quickest four-door sedans in the world without its speed limiter, but the car itself uses the same understated styling the brand is known for.

Aside from the usual M badges to signify this is a vehicle from the brand's lauded M Sport division, the car also adds larger air intakes, quad exhaust pipes and a small rear spoiler.

To help drivers make the most of the size and power of the BMW M5 the car uses electro-hydraulic steering for greater precision around corners.

Inside, the BMW is luxuriously-equipped and has space for four. The seats are decked out with leather and the huge range of equipment includes satnav, DAB radio and the traditional BMW head-up display.

Once out on the road, the BMW M5 can remind you of its turbocharged V8 by piping the sound through the car's speakers.

The car itself is incredibly refined and comfortable, particularly compared to the usual 200mph-plus supercars and a choice of driving modes can tweak suspension and steering to suit different driving conditions.

Drivers of the BMW M5 will also benefit from the brand's famed residual value and any investment in the super saloon will not be followed by dramatic depreciation.

SPECIFICATION

MANUFACTURE DATE	2011	**ENGINE**	4.4-litre V8 turbocharged petrol
WIDTH	1,891 mm	**TRANSMISSION**	Seven-speed, dual-clutch M DCT
HEIGHT	1,451 mm	**0-62 MPH**	3.7 seconds
LENGTH	4,910 mm	**POWER OUTPUT**	552 / bhp
MAXIMUM TORQUE	680 / nm	**BRAKES**	M carbon-ceramic brakes
MAXIMUM SPEED	205 mph	**SUSPENSION**	Double-wishbone at the front and multi-link suspension at the rear

LAMBORGHINI
REVENTON

The Lamborghini Reventon was the fastest roadster ever built when it arrived in 2009 in such limited numbers it also became one of the rarest of all time.

There is also a coupé version of the Reventon with similar design and performance figures but like the drop-top, numbers were limited to just 20 with an extra model being built for the Lamborghini museum.

The fierce, angular design is unmistakably from the Lamborghini stable and creates the impression of a fighter jet as opposed to a drop-top supercar.

In fact, the design of the carbon fibre body was actually inspired by a fighter jet and the razor-sharp lines are a mix of traditional Lamborghini design and that of the EuroFighter jets.

The Reventon even has a jet-style G-force meter on the dashboard showcasing the forces the driver is being subjected to when under acceleration.

The engine is equally fearsome. It comes in the form of a 6.5-litre V12 engine with 690bhp on tap and 660Nm of torque at 6000rpm and delivers breathtaking performance figures.

Where legal, the Lamborghini Reventon can reach a top speed of 205mph and acceleration from 0 to 62mph takes just 3.4 seconds. The noise produced by the V12 Lamborghini engine adds an intensity to the driving experience.

Driving a Reventon is a challenge in itself because of the car's wide turning circle and immense amount of power that can leave the wheels spinning.

Lamborghinis are traditionally considered to be wilder than some of their more refined supercar rivals and the Reventon is a car tuned to provide an intense driving experience. The engine is mounted in front of the rear axle with the transmission in front, putting more of the weight towards the rear of the car.

Open one of the two scissor doors and the interior is typically luxurious with leather and aluminium adorning the seats and instrument panel. There are two sports seats and in the convertible version, advanced roll bars that pop up in a fraction of a second if the car is flipped over.

SPECIFICATION

MANUFACTURE DATE	2008	**ENGINE**	6.5-litre V12 petrol
WIDTH	2,058 mm	**TRANSMISSION**	Six-speed manual
HEIGHT	1,135 mm	**0-62 MPH**	3.4 seconds
LENGTH	4,700 mm	**POWER OUTPUT**	690 / bhp
MAXIMUM TORQUE	660 / nm	**BRAKES**	Carbon Ceramic brakes
MAXIMUM SPEED	205 mph	**SUSPENSION**	Double-wishbones, electronically adjustable hydraulic shocks, anti-roll bars, anti-dive and anti-squat characteristics

MERCEDES-BENZ
SLR MCLAREN

Mercedes-Benz and McLaren are two of the biggest names in the automotive world. When they collaborate it invariably leads to high performance cars honed via both brands' F1 expertise.

The Mercedes-Benz SLR McLaren takes the standard SLR and injects a series of daunting performance figures courtesy of a 5.5-litre dry-sumped V8 engine with an output of 626bhp and 715Nm of torque.

Top speed is 207mph and the Mercedes SLR McLaren can reach 62mph in just 3.6 seconds. It takes 7.6 seconds to accelerate to 100mph and the quarter mile takes is over in 11.6 seconds.

The engine is matched to a five-speed automatic transmission and drivers can choose between three modes; Comfort for road driving, Sport for the track and Manual, where steering-mounted paddles are used to change gears for more control.

In manual mode, there are three additional modes to tweak the car's systems depending on driving conditions; the self-explanatory Sport, Supersport and Race modes ideal for track-based driving.

The use of carbon fibre throughout the body helps to keep down the weight of the SLR McLaren and improves performance in crash tests where carbon fibre outperforms more traditional materials.

The car also benefits from using the traditional SLR body which places the engine just behind the front wheels. However, it has been lowered compared to the standard SLR in order to provide a lower centre of gravity. This, in turn, improves the handling of the car.

The collaboration between Mercedes-Benz and McLaren lasted between 2004 and 2008 before McLaren decided to create its own range of supercars including the MP4-12C and the F1. At the same time, Mercedes developed the SLS AMG as its top-of-the-range supercar after the split.

In total, over 3,500 models were built at the assembly plant in England before production halted for the final time. A roadster version was also sold but was discontinued along with the coupé version in 2008.

SPECIFICATION

MANUFACTURE DATE	2004 - 2008	**ENGINE**	5.5-litre dry sumped V8 engine
WIDTH	1,908 mm	**TRANSMISSION**	Five-speed auto. Manual mode uses paddle shifters
HEIGHT	1,261 mm	**0-62 MPH**	3.6 seconds
LENGTH	4,656 mm	**POWER OUTPUT**	626 / bhp
MAXIMUM TORQUE	715 / nm	**BRAKES**	Sensotonic 'brake by wire' system. Carbon ceramic brake discs that are fade resistant to 1,200 degrees Celsius.
MAXIMUM SPEED	207 mph	**SUSPENSION**	Double-wishbone suspension at the front and rear made from forged aluminium

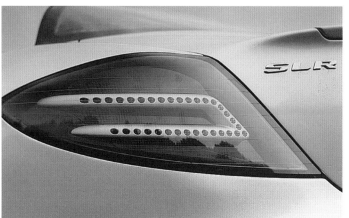

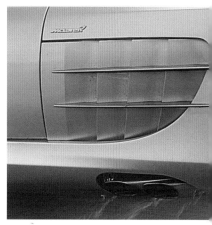

MCLAREN
MP4-12C

The McLaren MP4-12C was the car maker's triumphant return to road-legal cars after more than a decade focusing on its F1 team.

A major rival for the Ferrari 458 Italia, the McLaren MP4-12C has shunned the emotive design and heritage of its rival for a technical, precise supercar that demonstrates the cutting edge of such technology.

Everything from the carbon fibre composite chassis to the McLaren-designed engine has been carefully crafted to precise requirements.

The engine is a mid-mounted 3.8-litre twin-turbo V8 matched to a complex Seamless Shift seven-speed dual-clutch gearbox that boasts the ability to preselect the next gear by tapping the steering column-mounted paddles.

The engine develops 616bhp and can power the car to 62mph in a little over three seconds. There is 601Nm of torque on offer and 80 per cent of it is available at 2000rpm. Top speed is a blistering 207mph and it is capable of braking from 124mph in just five seconds.

The McLaren MP4-12C has been designed with impeccable manners around a track with precise, responsive steering helped along by electronics capable of adjusting the car's systems to improve control.

As a result the McLaren MP4-12C is a car that can be driven very easily and the power coming from the engine can push the car forward like very few other cars on the market.

The McLaren's ability to corner is bolstered by a one-part carbon fibre chassis that is the first of its kind in a production car. A Proactive Chassis Control system adapts the car's output to cope with the incredible levels of power and torque from the engine.

McLaren was heavily influenced by its successful F1 programme when it was designing the McLaren MP4-12C and a hydraulic anti-roll bar coupled with an advanced suspension setup comprising upper and lower wishbones helps to deliver a level of steering and control previously unseen on a supercar.

Inside, the McLaren is surprisingly comfortable with good all-round visibility which is a rarity in this segment and interior equipment includes Bluetooth, climate control and part-leather for the seats.

SPECIFICATION

MANUFACTURE DATE	2011	**ENGINE**	3.8-litre V8 petrol
WIDTH	2,909 mm	**TRANSMISSION**	Seven-speed manual dual clutch
HEIGHT	1,,199 mm	**0-62 MPH**	3.5 seconds
LENGTH	4,507 mm	**POWER OUTPUT**	626 / bhp
MAXIMUM TORQUE	601 / nm	**BRAKES**	Steel brakes as standard Ceramic brakes are an optional extra
MAXIMUM SPEED	207 mph	**SUSPENSION**	Adaptive suspension featuring hydraulic links to adapt to the road conditions

PORSCHE CARRERA GT

The Porsche Carrera GT is one of the most performance-focused Porsche models to grace the roads. Built between 2004 and 2007, the Carrera GT is capable of speeds of up to 209mph.

A mid-engine, rear-wheel drive car, the Porsche Carrera GT pushes an incredible amount of power to its back wheels. The 5.7-litre V10 engine delivers an output of 612bhp at 8000rpm and is matched to a lightweight ceramic clutch capable of coping with up to 16000rpm.

The Porsche Carrera GT can hit speeds of 209mph and the 0-62mph sprint time is 3.9 seconds. It can go on to reach 100mph from standing in just 6.8 seconds.

While the clutch is incredibly advanced, its size and weight also means the car is particularly easy to stall for those who use it on a daily basis – a unique challenge for owners of this supercar.

The Porsche Carrera GT is a technical masterpiece and every aspect of the car is designed to improve performance and driving dynamics.

For example, the rear spoiler creates 400kg of down force and even with all that power going to the rear wheels, steering and handling is sharp even at higher speeds.

However, towards the top end of its performance the Carrera GT can be a challenge to control – all the electronic driving aids can only do so much for a car capable of travelling over 200mph.

Inside the Porsche Carrera GT there is typical Porsche luxury with quality materials used throughout and plenty of equipment including a Bose audio system and a bespoke satnav system as standard.

In terms of design, the Porsche Carrera GT is one of the more subtle Porsche models. However, its simple, clean styling is entirely functional and includes large air vents for the V10 engine and a sleek, aerodynamic silhouette to improve performance.

At its launch, the full production run of over 1,200 had sold almost instantly, making the Carrera GT one of the most popular supercars of all time from a single production run. It was initially built after Porsche had abandoned its 2000 Le Mans programme, using the same engine from its concept.

SPECIFICATION

MANUFACTURE DATE	2004-2007	ENGINE	5.7-litre V10 petrol
WIDTH	1,921 mm	TRANSMISSION	Six-speed manual
HEIGHT	1,166 mm	0-62 MPH	3.9 seconds
LENGTH	4,613 mm	POWER OUTPUT	612 / bhp
MAXIMUM TORQUE	640 / nm	BRAKES	Porsche Ceramic Composite Brake (PCCB)
MAXIMUM SPEED	209 mph	SUSPENSION	Pushrod suspension with double track control arms

FAST CARS
210-230
MPH

LAMBORGHINI
DIABLO GT

Lamborghini debuted the Diablo GT at the 1999 Geneva Motor Show, intending the supercar to be a strictly limited-edition model that was built using the manufacturer's experience of producing a GT2 race car, combining the company's experience of producing high-performance road cars.

The result was a high-performance supercar capable of trackday histrionics while being a viable car for the open roads. For a time, the Diablo GT could also stake a claim to being the fastest production car in the world, with a top speed of 211mph.

The Diablo GT used a then-new Lamborghini V12 6.0-litre engine with a wider front track, improved chassis and suspension and lighter kerbweight. The 5.7-litre engine from the Diablo was redesigned and uprated to 6.0 litres and power increased to 575bhp with torque at 630Nm. The transmission was the same five-speed from the Diablos, but buyers could specify gear ratios. An enlarged front track, improved suspension and tubular frame gave a more stable ride at very high speeds.

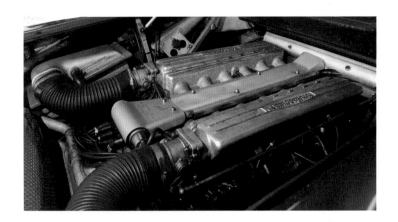

The cars were fitted with radically altered aggressive bodywork, a stripped-down interior and an enlarged engine. Exterior changes from the Diablo included a black carbon fibre front air scoop, large brake ducts and a wider track. A carbon fibre diffuser and large centre-mounted exhaust pipes were added at the rear. The radical new body was composed mostly of carbon fibre, with the steel roof and aluminium doors being the only components to retain their standard material.

Inside were carbon fibre panels, race-specification bucket seats with four-point seatbelt harnesses and a smaller steering wheel. Nods to the supposed everyday nature of the Diablo GT meant that satnav, rear parking cameras and air conditioning were available.

Only 80 examples were produced for sale.

SPECIFICATION

MANUFACTURE DATE	1990 - 2001	**ENGINE**	V12 6.0-litre engine
WIDTH	2,040 mm	**TRANSMISSION**	Lamborghini five-speed + reverse manual all-synchromesh, ZF final drive with limited-slip differential
HEIGHT	1,105 mm	**0-62 MPH**	3.9 seconds
LENGTH	4,460 mm	**POWER OUTPUT**	575 / bhp
MAXIMUM TORQUE	630 / nm	**BRAKES**	Brembo servo-assisted four-wheel disc brakes, 330 mm front × 284 mm rear)
MAXIMUM SPEED	211 mph	**SUSPENSION**	Independent front & rear with parallelogram action unequal length control arms, anti-roll bar, one coil shock unit at the front two coils at the rear axle

LAMBORGHINI
MURCIÉLAGO
LP640

Introduced in 2006, the Lamborghini Murciélago LP640 model was designed as a spiritual successor to the Countach. The LP640 tag refers to the placement of the engine – Longitudinale Posteriore – and the amount of horsepower the engine can develop.

The Lamborghini Murciélago LP640 also benefited from a larger front spoiler and larger air intakes, with a huge centre-mounted exhaust. LED taillights, Hermera wheels and a glass-louvered engine cover were all new.

The Lamborghini V12 engine displaced 6.5 litres and power went up to 640bhp at 8000rpm. A six-speed gearbox incorporated a thrust mode on the optional e-Gear transmission, resulting in ultra-fast launches and a 60mph sprint time of 3.3 seconds. The quarter-mile took 11.2 seconds at 127mph.

Inside, the Lamborghini Murciélago LP640 boasted a satnav system, 140-litre trunk and the list of options was almost limitless, with bespoke interiors decided by buyers. Despite these touches, however, entry remained via roof-hinged doors and the V12 was another indication of the LP640's intent.

At the red line of 8000rpm the Murciélago has a fearsome roar, with 631bhp available from the 6.5-litre V12, which develops maximum torque of 660Nm at 5000rpm.

300 units were sold, though a Roadster version and a SuperVeloce model for the track followed. A Lamborghini Murciélago LP640 Versace was a limited-edition model available in either white or black: only 20 were produced as both coupés and roadsters while custom interiors were finished in two-toned Versace leather, and included Versace luggage, driving shoes and gloves.

SPECIFICATION

MANUFACTURE DATE	2006	ENGINE	V12, 6496cc, 48v
WIDTH	2,045 mm	TRANSMISSION	Single-plate six-speed manual
HEIGHT	1,135 mm	0-62 MPH	3.3 seconds
LENGTH	4,580 mm	POWER OUTPUT	631 / bhp @ 8,000 rpm
MAXIMUM TORQUE	660 / nm @ 6,000 rpm	BRAKES	Porsche 380mm front x 355mm rear discs with four channel ABS
MAXIMUM SPEED	213 mph	SUSPENSION	Independent double-wishbone, anti-roll bar, anti-dive & anti-squat

PAGANI
ZONDA F

The Pagani Zonda F supercar paid tribute to founder Horacio Pagani and Formula One world champion race driver Juan Manuel Fangio. As such, it was intended to show a commitment to lightness, performance and innovation and the Zonda F sported a logo, design concept and name dedicated to Fangio.

Built alongside its regular production model, the Zonda F is a special edition supercar which was refined to produce a more appealing supercar package. The changes resulted in a lighterweight, faster and more powerful car.

The resulting supercar is powered by a mid-mounted, longitudinal 7.3-litre V12 petrol engine with sequential multipoint injection that can output 594bhp and develop 780Nm of torque. The commitment to low kerbweight means extensive use of carbon fibre, titanium and aluminium.

Exhaust manifolds are designed in compliance with the Formula 1 standards and the use of the powerful Mercedes-AMG engine and lightweight engineering means a power-to-weight ratio of 529bhp/ton. Aerodynamics were also improved with the addition of a revised front end, new rear spoiler and more aerodynamic vents all around.

The Zonda F was equipped with an extra headlight and different fog lights at the sides, new bodywork and different side mirrors. Options included carbon and ceramic brakes developed in conjunction with Brembo, magnesium wheels and a chassis reengineered to improve rigidity and reduce weight.

The Zonda F sprints to 60mph in 3.6 seconds and 124mph (200kmh) in 9.8 seconds but can brake from 124mph to zero in 4.4 seconds, the awesome stopping ability courtesy of massive brake discs also available as optional ceramic discs to eradicate brake fade.

Production of the Pagani Zonda F was limited to 25 cars, though 25 examples were produced of the drop-top Zonda F Roadster.

SPECIFICATION

MANUFACTURE DATE	2005	**ENGINE**	V12, Mid-mounted, longitudinal V12 7.3-litre petrol engine with sequential multipoint injection
WIDTH	2,055 mm	**TRANSMISSION**	Six-speed manual gearbox, rear-wheel drive, limited-slip differential
HEIGHT	1,141 mm	**0-62 MPH**	3.6 seconds
LENGTH	4,435 mm	**POWER OUTPUT**	594 / bhp @ 6,200rpm
MAXIMUM TORQUE	780 / nm @ 4,000rpm	**BRAKES**	Ventilated carbon-ceramic discs, 380mm front and rear
MAXIMUM SPEED	214 mph	**SUSPENSION**	Double-wishbones, coil springs, dampers, anti-roll bar front and rear

FERRARI
ENZO

Ferrari has produced a handful of cars that represent the pinnacle of the Italian manufacturer's technological abilities. The Ferrari Enzo was one such car, hitting roads in 2002 and benefiting from Ferrari's Formula One and road-car experience at a time when Ferrari was ruling F1 with Michael Schumacher at the wheel of its racing cars.

O ne example is the car's advanced aerodynamics, with downforce that reached a maximum of 775 kg at 300km/h. The Enzo's front section was inspired by the Formula 1 car's nose cone, while Pininfarina was tasked with the job of ensuring a striking design that paid homage to classic Ferrari styling. The car's dashboard and interface are influenced by motor sport too, while weight-saving is represented by a composite bodywork and a carbon fibre and aluminium honeycomb sandwich chassis to keep down weight.

The Enzo is powered by a 6.0-litre V12 that, at the time, was a completely new 12-cylinder engine which drew on Ferrari's F1 experience. With a maximum power output of 660bhp at 7800 rpm and maximum torque of 657Nm at 5500rpm, the Enzo was capable of blistering power, huge torque at low revs and a broad range of use. The top speed is 217mph and the 60mph sprint takes just over 3.6 seconds.

The Enzo's rear-mounted F1 gearbox was connected directly to the engine to cut gearshifting times down to 150 milliseconds. Meanwhile, with all that power and torque on tap, a specially-developed system from Brembo featured Carbon-Ceramic Material discs, the first time these had been used on a Ferrari road car despite having been employed for years by the Scuderia in Formula 1.

Just 400 examples were built of the Enzo and the car remains a landmark in supercar history.

SPECIFICATION

MANUFACTURE DATE	2002	**ENGINE**	Rear, longitudinal 65° 6.0-litre V12
WIDTH	2,035 mm	**TRANSMISSION**	Electro-hydraulic F1 6-speed
HEIGHT	1,147 mm	**0-62 MPH**	3.65 seconds
LENGTH	4,702 mm	**POWER OUTPUT**	660 / bhp @ 7,800 rpm
MAXIMUM TORQUE	657 / nm @ 5,500 rpm	**BRAKES**	Carbon-ceramic discs
MAXIMUM SPEED	217 mph	**SUSPENSION**	Independent push-rod, unequal-length wishbones, coil springs, telescopic shock absorbers with electronic adaptive damping

PAGANI
ZONDA CINQUE ROADSTER

With a production limited to only 5 cars, the Pagani Zonda Cinque Roadster is powered by a Mercedes AMG V12 engine producing 678bhp, hits 62mph from a standstill in just 3.4 seconds and tops out at 217mph. Stopping distances from 124mph were an eye-watering 4.3 seconds courtesy of carbon-ceramic brake discs.

The Zonda Cinque Roadster's twin-turbocharged engine transmits power through a sequential six-speed transmission and a range of electrical controls from Bosch including a traction control system to combat the acres of power and torque on offer.

Changes over and above the standard Zonda on the Cinque – Italian for five – include a stronger chassis, formed from a type of carbon fibre with threads of titanium woven into it, to stiffen the chassis when the roof is removed.

The striking Cinque features a remarkable rear too, with a redesigned exhaust that has also been completely redesigned and there are a number of additional carbon fibre intakes and fins all over the car.

An adjustable suspension means that the car can be set up differently for a range of driving conditions, including fast-shifting track driving; the interior features carbon fibre racing seats.

The chassis is a carbon-titanium monocoque for strength and lightness: a magnesium suspension, carbon fibre brake discs and magnesium alloy wheels contribute to a dry weight of 1210kg – a massive 70kg lighter than the original Zonda S Roadster.

With only five ever built and an original price tag of over $2 million, you'll count yourself lucky to ever see one on the roads. Nevertheless the Pagani Zonda Cinque Roadster remains an irresistible example of hypercar exotica.

SPECIFICATION

MANUFACTURE DATE	2010	**ENGINE**	Twin turbocharged V12 Mercedes Benz AMG engine V12
WIDTH	2,055 mm	**TRANSMISSION**	Gearbox: Cima six-speed sequential gearbox
HEIGHT	1,151 mm	**0-62 MPH**	3.4 seconds
LENGTH	4,395 mm	**POWER OUTPUT**	678 / bhp
MAXIMUM TORQUE	780 / nm	**BRAKES**	380mm Brembo brakes in carbon-ceramic; self ventilated with hydraulic servo brake
MAXIMUM SPEED	217 mph	**SUSPENSION**	Double-wishbones, pull rod actuated coil springs, Ohlins adjustable shock absorbers, anti-roll bar

LAMBORGHINI
AVENTADOR
LP 700-4

The Lamborghini Aventador LP 700–4 is a two-door, two-seater supercar that replaced the Murciélago in 2011 as the flagship model in the Lamborghini lineup. Needless to say, it's another Lamborghini named after a famed fighting bull – and the all-new V12 petrol engine is reassuringly powerful.

With a 6.5-litre V12 mated to a seven-speed ISR semi-automatic transmission, the Aventador is capable of a phenomenal 690bhp at 8,250rpm, with maximum torque of 690Nm at 5,500rpm. Those figures mean a top speed of 217mph and spine-crushing acceleration – 60mph in 2.9 seconds. The V12's power-to-weight ratio is 426bhp per ton and the quarter-mile take a mere 10.6 seconds, by which time the Aventador is travelling at 137mph.

The single-clutch seven-speed semi-automatic is capable of shift in just 50 milliseconds while an all-wheel drive system from Haldex boosts traction and dynamic handling capacity with almost 700Nm of torque on tap. The Aventador is commonly held to be the most drivable Lamborghini ever, in contrast with the usual reputation of Lamborghini cars as brutally quick and dangerous for unwary drivers.

The Lamborghini flagship uses a carbon fibre monocoque that is twice as stiff as the Murciélago even though it is lighter and more powerful. In terms of the Murciélago, the Aventador is slightly longer and narrower though it remains the same height.

The Aventador has a number of driver-specified features, such as a rear spoiler that can be set in three 3 positions depending on speed and drive select mode; ESP/ ABS with different ESP characteristics; steering and differential managed by drive select mode with three modes.

Endlessly customisable inside, the Aventador boasts the startling looks and power that Lamborghini is known for – and marries something of the outlook of a grand tourer. It's the most complete sports car that Lamborghini has ever made.

SPECIFICATION

MANUFACTURE DATE	2011	**ENGINE**	6.5-litre V12
WIDTH	2,030 mm	**TRANSMISSION**	Seven-speed ISR Semi-auto
HEIGHT	1,136 mm	**0-62 MPH**	2.9 seconds
LENGTH	4,780 mm	**POWER OUTPUT**	690 / bhp @ 8250 rpm
MAXIMUM TORQUE	690 / nm @ 5,500 rpm	**BRAKES**	Dual hydraulic circuit brake system, 400mm 6-cylinder brake calipers at front, 380mm 4-cylinder brake calipers at rear
MAXIMUM SPEED	217 mph	**SUSPENSION**	Front and rear horizontal monotube damper with push-rod system

MCLAREN
P1

The McLaren P1 is a rarity – a hybrid supercar that uses a petrol-electric powertrain to attain speeds in excess of 200mph.

The concept car debuted at the 2012 Paris Motor Show and represents McLaren Automotive's long-awaited successor to the legendary McLaren F1. McLaren claims the car will have a top speed of 217.5mph and will reach 186mph in under 17 seconds. The P1 is believed to be capable of speeds nearing 239 mph, but the car will be electronically limited to 217 mph. Acceleration from a standing start means that the P1 can hit 60mph in under three seconds and 186mph (300kmh) in under 17 seconds.

With a powertrain that uses technology and know-how from Formula One, the P1 will be powered by a revised version of the 3.8-litre twin-turbo V8 petrol engine used in the McLaren MP4-12C, tuned to 727bhp.

The engine will work in tandem with a 176bhp Kinetic Energy Regeneration System (KERS) similar to the kinds used in F1 that recover power that would otherwise be lost while braking. This hybrid powertrain is connected to a seven-speed dual-clutch transmission and, combined, will mean the P1 has a total power output of just over 900bhp at 7500 rpm and a maximum torque figure of 900Nm – figures that are virtually unmatched outside the rarest of hypercar exotica.

The powertrain can run using either the petrol V8 by itself or with the electric motor. Like mainstream hybrid road cars, electrical power is stored in batteries and the P1 can be charged via plug-in equipment. Unlike road cars the stored energy can be used to deliver a KERS-like boost in performance; an Instant Power Assist System will provide a boost to the petrol engine via the electric motor. The concept car debuted at the 2012 Paris Motor Show and represents McLaren Automotive's long-awaited successor to the legendary McLaren F1. McLaren claims the car will have a top speed of 217.5mph and will reach 186mph in under 17 seconds. The P1 is believed to be capable of speeds nearing 239 mph, but the car will be electronically limited to 217 mph. Acceleration from a standing start means that the P1 can hit 60mph in under three seconds and hits 186mph (300kmh) in under 17 seconds.

With a powertrain that uses technology and know-how from Formula One, the P1 will be powered by a revised version of the 3.8-litre twin-turbo V8 petrol engine used in the McLaren MP4-12C, tuned to 727bhp.

The engine will work in tandem with a 176bhp Kinetic Energy Regeneration System (KERS) similar to the kinds used in F1 that recover power that would otherwise be lost while braking. This hybrid powertrain is connected to a seven-speed dual-clutch transmission and, combined, will mean the P1 has a total power output of just over 900bhp at 7500 rpm and a maximum torque figure of 900Nm – figures that are virtually unmatched outside the rarest of hypercar exotica.

The powertrain can run using either the petrol V8 by itself or with the electric motor. Like mainstream hybrid road cars, electrical power is stored in batteries and the P1 can be charged via plug-in equipment. Unlike road cars the stored energy can be used to deliver a KERS-like boost in performance; an Instant Power Assist System will provide an instant boost to the petrol engine via the electric motor.

Another F1 innovation will be a Drag Reduction System (DRS), which operates the car's rear wing to eliminate downforce in straight lines. Carbon-ceramic brakes provide stopping power and styling will largely be influenced by the McLaren MP4-12C supercar, with a carbon fibre monocoque and roof structure safety cage concept called MonoCage.

Four driving modes will be selectable – normal, sport, track and race – while the whole suspension can be raised by 50mm at speeds of up to 37mph for city driving.

No more than 375 cars will be produced, all fully equipped for road and track. Every model will cost in excess of $1m and the car will battle against LaFerrari for mainstream hypercar supremacy.

SPECIFICATION

MANUFACTURE DATE	2013	**ENGINE**	McLaren M838T twin-turbo 3.8 L V8 with KERS facility
WIDTH	2,946 mm	**TRANSMISSION**	Seven-speed dual-clutch
HEIGHT	1,170 mm	**0-62 MPH**	3.0 seconds
LENGTH	4,585 mm	**POWER OUTPUT**	727 / bhp
MAXIMUM TORQUE	900 / nm	**BRAKES**	Le Mans-spec 390mm front brake discs with six-piston calipers, and 380mm rear brakes with four-piston calipers
MAXIMUM SPEED	217 mph	**SUSPENSION**	Nitrogen-filled carbon-fibre accumulator self-levelling system

FERRARI
LAFERRARI

Not one hybrid hypercar, but two. With the McLaren P1 unveiled in 2012, Ferrari followed up shortly afterwards with LaFerrari, unveiled at the 2013 Geneva Motor Show.

The car, also known by the codename F70, is a limited-edition petrol-electric supercar that uses a KERS-like Formula One boost system providing the highest power output of any Ferrari whilst decreasing fuel consumption by 40 percent.

The LaFerrari's V12 petrol engine displaces 6.3 litres and has a power output of 789bhp, supplemented by a 163bhp HY-KERS system that provides overboost similar to that of a turbocharger. The LaFerrari has a top speed of 217mph and a sprint time of under three seconds; with 190mph possible from a standing start in under 15 seconds.

The V12 is mid-mounted and mated to an F1 dual-clutch gearbox with power going to the rear wheels. The resulting high levels of torque reach 900Nm and the powertrain revs up to the 9,250rpm limit.

The hybrid supercar has a dry weight of just 1,255kg and is built on a carbon fibre monocoque structure developed with 27 percent more torsional rigidity and 22 percent more beam stiffness than the Enzo. Carbon ceramic Brembo discs provide the stopping power.

Active aerodynamics include a front diffuser, underbody guide vane, rear diffuser and rear wing – leading to the best aerodynamic efficiency of any Ferrari. Electronic wizardry has been ported from Ferrari's Formula One programme and include an F1 electronic traction and stability control, a third-generation electronic differential and magnetorheological damping that adjust the ride depending on conditions.

Ferrari says that only 499 units of the supercar will be built, while styling will be undertaken in-house by Ferrari – the first prancing horse not to have any styling input from Pininfarina since 1951. Prices will start at around $1.3m.

SPECIFICATION

MANUFACTURE DATE	2013	**ENGINE**	6.3-litre V12 with electric motor and KERS
WIDTH	1,992 mm	**TRANSMISSION**	Seven-speed dual-clutch automated manual
HEIGHT	1,116 mm	**0-62 MPH**	3.0 seconds
LENGTH	4,702 mm	**POWER OUTPUT**	789 / bhp + 163 / bhp
MAXIMUM TORQUE	900 / nm	**BRAKES**	Carbon ceramic Brembo discs on the front (398mm) and rear (380mm)
MAXIMUM SPEED	217 mph	**SUSPENSION**	Double-wishbone front suspension, multi-link rear suspension

ASTON MARTIN
ONE-77

Aston Martin's One-77 is the fastest model the British manufacturer has ever produced, using a 7.3-litre V12 to propel the limited-edition supercar to 220mph. The 0–60mph sprint takes 3.5 seconds.

This naturally-aspirated engine was the most powerful of its kind at the time – producing 750bhp and 750Nm of torque – through a strengthened version of the Aston Martin DB9's six-speed automated manual transmission.

The One-77's lightweight chassis is constructed using only carbon fibre, while body panels are aluminium. As a result, the two-seater coupé weighs 1,630kg. Active areodynamics including an adjustable spoiler, splitters and a diffuser, ensure downforce to improve traction, as does a limited-slip differential to aid cornering.

As befits the price tag of around $1.5m, the One-77 is a high-specification machine, with a leather-trimmed sports steering wheel, electrically adjustable lightweight memory seats, glass switchgear, LED headlights, touch-sensitive buttons and parking sensors. Much of the car's relative proportions observe the so-called 'golden ratio' that recurs throughout geometry, nature and mathematics and was widely used in Ancient Greek architecture.

The One-77 is shorter than the DB9, lower than even the Vantage and has an extremely wide track that's only slightly narrower than a Hummer H1 SUV. The engine is mounted 100mm lower than in any previous V12-engined Aston, which helps keep the One-77's centre-of-gravity very low.

This Aston hypercar also features a new Dynamic Suspension Spool Valve which ensures that dampers are fully adjustable. Owners were able to specify their chosen set-up characteristics, meaning that the One-77 could be ordered as a grand tourer or a track weapon – and everything in between.

As the name suggests, just 77 versions of the car were built – bespoke for every individual customer – with an asking price of close to £1.15 million. At those prices, there are very few realistic competitors, with the Bugatti Veyron an obvious rival. But for hypercar power and performance and classic British elegance, the One-77 is exclusive, classy and super-quick.

SPECIFICATION

MANUFACTURE DATE	2009	ENGINE	7.3-litre petrol V12
WIDTH	2,204 mm	TRANSMISSION	Six-speed automated manual
HEIGHT	1,222 mm	0-62 MPH	3.7 seconds
LENGTH	4,601 mm	POWER OUTPUT	750 / bhp
MAXIMUM TORQUE	750 / nm	BRAKES	Carbon Ceramic Matrix brakes
MAXIMUM SPEED	220 mph	SUSPENSION	Height-adjustable pushrod suspension coupled with dynamic stability control

LAMBORGHINI
VENENO

The Lamborghini Veneno is a strictly limited-edition hypercar from the Sant'Agata Bolognese manufacturer. It was first exhibited during the 2013 Geneva Motor Show and is built to celebrate Lamborghini's 50th anniversary.

B ased on the Lamborghini Aventador, the prototype, called Car Zero, is a showcar finished in grey and includes an Italian flag vinyl on both sides of the car. Production will be limited to three models in green, white and red to represent the colours of the Italian flag – the name Veneno means venom in Spanish and Portuguese; as is traditional the Lamborghini is named after a particularly vicious bull.

The engine is a development of the Aventador's 6.5 L V12 and produces 740bhp. The Veneno is 275 pounds lighter than the Aventador, so the 60mph time takes just 2.8 seconds and maximum speed is 221mph. The engine is mated to an ISR manual gearbox and permanent all-wheel drive, both of which are specially-adapted to the Veneno.

Those performance figures and the power-to-weight ratio of 1.93 kg/bhp are aided by the Veneno's lightweight design. Carbon fibre dominates the interior of the Veneno, too. The carbon fibre monocoque becomes visible inside the car around the central tunnel and the sills. Meanwhile, the two lightweight bucket seats are made from Lamborghini's patented Forged Composite and the lightweight woven carbon fibre CarbonSkin is used to clad the entire cockpit, part of the seats and the headliner. A new feature is the G-meter, which provides information on G-forces experienced by the driver while cornering.

The Veneno has been optimized for aerodynamics and high speed cornering stability, with a smooth underbody, substantial diffuser and splitter to increase the level of downforce and aid cornering performance. The rear lights feature a Y-shaped design, while the engine cover features six wedge-shaped openings that help cool the V12 engine.

The car's front features an aerodynamic wing with large channels that allow the air to arrive in the front hood, wheels and front of the windshield.

The three production cars cost around $4m and are all spoken for, two of which are believed to be heading for the USA.

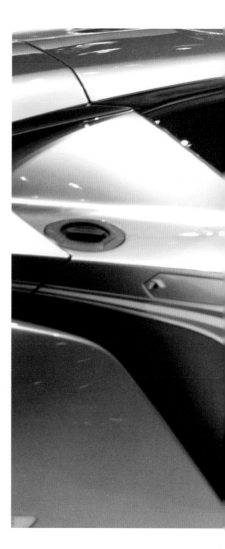

SPECIFICATION

MANUFACTURE DATE	2013	ENGINE	6.5-litre V12
WIDTH	TBA	TRANSMISSION	Seven-speed Semi-auto transmission with all-wheel drive
HEIGHT	TBA	0-62 MPH	2.8 seconds
LENGTH	TBA	POWER OUTPUT	740 / bhp
MAXIMUM TORQUE	700 / nm @ 6,750 rpm	BRAKES	Carbon-ceramic brake discs
MAXIMUM SPEED	221 mph	SUSPENSION	Racing chassis with pushrod suspension and horizontal spring/damper units

GUMPERT
APOLLO

The Gumpert Apollo is hardly a subtle supercar. One of the most striking fast cars in the world – and blessed with one of the more unusual names – the Apollo was conceived by former Audi manager and motorsport honcho Roland Gumpert and uses an Audi-sourced twin-turbo V8, with power output as high as 780bhp and top speed of up to 224mph.

T he powerful V8 has 40 valves, updated rods and pistons to cope with the awesome power created by two turbochargers strapped onto the engine. Peak power arrives at 6800rpm while maximum torque of 597lb-ft is developed at 5000rpm.

The body, such as it is, is composed of fibre glass or carbon fibre, so weight is kept to a minimum – the Apollo weighs a paltry 1100kg as a result, meaning a power-to-weight ratio of a staggering 583bhp per ton with the lower-rated 641bhp model. Meanwhile, the Gumpert's aerodynamics are so effective that it can theoretically be driven upside-down in a tunnel at the higher end of the speed band, such is the downforce created by the car's spoiler and splitter.

SPECIFICATION

MANUFACTURE DATE	2005	**ENGINE**	4.2-litre V8
WIDTH	1,998 mm	**TRANSMISSION**	Six-speed sequential manual
HEIGHT	1,114 mm	**0-62 MPH**	3.1 seconds
LENGTH	4,460 mm	**POWER OUTPUT**	641 / bhp
MAXIMUM TORQUE	809 / nm	**BRAKES**	380mm discs on all wheels
MAXIMUM SPEED	224 mph	**SUSPENSION**	Double-wishbone suspension with adjustable rebound and compression. It also has a front anti-roll bar and a titanium rear anti-roll bar

Doors hinge from the middle of the roof and the big wheels arches enter into the cabin. Despite the Apollo being built to be used on the road, the interior belies its track-day appeal, with a minimalist carbon fibre interior with buckets seats and rows of dials which are designed to feed back information on the car's dynamics and performance.

Most Apollos come with a sequential stick for changing gear – another feature most frequently seen in cars designed to be used to their full potential.

While technically a road car, the Apollo's hyper performance puts it almost beyond supercar status. Its screaming acceleration, enormous power-to-weight ratio and massive top speed put it virtually in a league of its own.

BRISTOL
FIGHTER T

If supercars were a simple matter of power, torque and speed there are few that can top the Bristol Fighter T.

Powered by a twin-turbo 8-litre V10 with 1,012bhp and a massive 1,400Nm of torque, the Fighter T has an official top speed of 225mph. However, Bristol claimed that their car was theoretically capable of a scarcely believable 270mph.

The reasoning behind the limited top figure was safety, with stability and power transfer a problem for motorcars above certain speeds, with few drivetrains able to withstand such ferocious power - the six-speed manual gearbox was able to handle 60mph in first gear alone.

Nevertheless, the Fighter T could manage 60mph in 3.4 seconds from the modified Chrysler V10 engine, which had two turbochargers strapped to it. A very impressive drag coefficient of 0.27 aided the Fighter T's performance too, as did a kerbweight of around 1500kg – extremely low for such a fast car.

The lack of any driver aids or even an airbag made the Fighter T a rather eccentric car. It was very much in keeping with the company, which disavowed press interest and has just one showroom, located in London's swanky Kensington. Despite a flirtation with bankruptcy in 2011, the company still builds cars by hand at a volume thought to be less than three figures per annum.

Bristol's motto of 'Nicely Understated, Never Underrated' might
have been debatable given the hyperbolic performance. However,
the reasonably subtle exterior – apart from the gullwing doors – and
interior styling put it strongly at odds with the majority of hypercar
exotica. This grand tourer was not only tall, it was narrow, giving it
an elegance rarely seen in today's cars but making it reasonably
drivable in the urban environment, too.

Regardless of its eccentricity, the Bristol Fighter T remains one of
the fastest production cars ever built.

SPECIFICATION

MANUFACTURE DATE	2009	**ENGINE**	V10 Twin Turbo 7,994 cc
WIDTH	1,795 mm	**TRANSMISSION**	Six-speed manual
HEIGHT	1,345 mm	**0-62 MPH**	3.5 seconds
LENGTH	4,420 mm	**POWER OUTPUT**	1012 / bhp @ 5,000 rpm
MAXIMUM TORQUE	1,405 / nm @ 4,500 rpm	**BRAKES**	Vented Discs with 6-Piston calipers front; 4-piston at rear
MAXIMUM SPEED	225 mph	**SUSPENSION**	Coil- sprung double-wishbone suspension with anti-roll bars front and rear

NOBLE
M600

Noble's M600 supercar combines the best of both worlds – modern carbon-fibre composite across a handbuilt chassis; awesome power and torque with sumptuous interiors.

The M600 weighs just 1250kg and uses a Yamaha V8 twin-turbo petrol engine sending 650bhp at 6800rpm and 819Nm of torque at 3800rpm to the rear wheels, though the variable boost available allows drivers to select power rating via a dial on the dashboard.

The Road setting provides 450bhp, Track gives 550bhp, and Race gives the full boost pressure and 650bhp. The Yamaha is given quite the makeover to be able to withstand all that power and torque – with beefed-up conrods, pistons beefed-up crankshafts.

A top speed of 225mph and a 0-60mph sprint time of 3.5 seconds, a 0-100 mph time of 6.5 seconds and 0-200mph time of under 30 seconds are possible as a result. The standing quarter mile takes 11 seconds flat and the combination of power and low weight means a power-to-weight ratio of 541bhp per ton.

Inside, the Noble M600 is a mix of leather or Alcantara upholstery and wool carpets, while seats are built using carbon fibre composite. Each M600 includes a unique identification plate and the car can be specced according to the driver's preferences.

The amount of electronic assistance technology on the M600 was limited, the theory being that the car will reward good drivers; without ABS the car is certainly not for novice drivers, though it remains a supercar that draws considerable praise for its raw ability and engaging manner.

With performance figures that rival and, in some cases, exceed those of the Bugatti Veyron and other hypercars, the M600 shows that British cars can still mix it with the fastest and most powerful supercars in the world.

SPECIFICATION

MANUFACTURE DATE	2010	**ENGINE**	4.4 litre V8 twin-turbo
WIDTH	1,910 mm	**TRANSMISSION**	Six-speed manual
HEIGHT	1,140 mm	**0-62 MPH**	3.5 seconds
LENGTH	4,360 mm	**POWER OUTPUT**	650 / bhp
MAXIMUM TORQUE	819 / nm	**BRAKES** Six-piston calipers front; four-piston calipers	rear on Speedline-manufacturer wheels
MAXIMUM SPEED	225 mph	**SUSPENSION**	Double-wishbone coil springs, dampers, anti-roll bar

JAGUAR
XJ220

A car that hailed back to the glorious motorsport days of garagistas, the Jaguar XJ200 was a supercar that originated from an unofficial club within Jaguar Engineering with a view to emulating Jaguar's halcyon racing days.

Equipped with a heavily-modified 3.5-litre V6 542bhp at 7000rpm and 645Nm of torque at 4500rpm, it was also the first Jaguar engine to use forced induction, using two Garrett turbochargers. The XJ220 was renowned for its high levels of torque from low revs and also ensured a peculiarly efficient supercar, with over 30mpg theoretically possible.

The chassis used an aluminium honeycomb construction for high torsional stiffness and light weight – the XJ200 tipping the scales at a relatively low 1456kg, meaning a power-to-weight ratio of 372bhp per tonne.

Aerodynamics were harnessed to increase downforce, with underbody and venturi used to generate such downforce that the car could be driven upside down, in theory. The high torque on offer meant that only a five-speed gearbox was required, though an extra-strong syncromesh was required for launch starts.

Inside, the XJ220 was reasonably suave, with full leather and an Alpine stereo inside, though part-sharing meant that some switchgear was borrowed from Jaguar's then-owners, Ford.

The recession of the early 90s put paid to the XJ220 as a viable contender to Ferrari, McLaren and others – only 281 were ever built – and marked Jaguar's last meaningful attempt at building a supercar. However, as a car that was genuinely quick and a super drive – as evident by its holding the Nurburgring production car lap record for eight years – it goes down in history as a glorious example of modern British volume supercar manufacturing.

SPECIFICATION

MANUFACTURE DATE	1989 -1992	**ENGINE**	3.5-litre V6 quad cam with twin Garrett T3 turbochargers
WIDTH	2,007 mm	**TRANSMISSION**	FF Developments five-speed transaxle with AP Racing 8.5-in diameter lug drive clutch
HEIGHT	1,151 mm	**0-62 MPH**	3.6 seconds
LENGTH	4,930 mm	**POWER OUTPUT**	542 / bhp @ 7,000 rpm
MAXIMUM TORQUE	644 / nm @ 4,500 rpm	**BRAKES**	Ventilated discs 330mm front, 300mm rear; AP Racing four-pot calipers all round
MAXIMUM SPEED	227 mph	**SUSPENSION**	Front and rear: independent with double unequal-length wishbones, inboard coil springs, Bilstein gas-pressurised dampers and anti-roll bars

FAST CARS
230-260
MPH

TVR

CEBERA SPEED 12

Chances are, most car enthusiasts will have never seen the TVR Speed 12 after its promising development was halted before it could ever make it onto the road.

Designed in Blackpool, England, the TVR Speed 12 was a project that aimed to create the fastest production car in the world, back in 1997.

Based on the TVR GT1 Class Le Mans racer the TVR Speed 12 used a 7.7-litre, 12-cylinder engine reportedly delivering over 1,000bhp. With a four-figure power output and a lightweight architecture, top speed was expected to hit 240mph.

TVR boasted the car would be a rival to the McLaren F1, one of the fastest cars on sale at the time, even quoting faster times than its illustrious rival.

However, these figures were only estimates and tests on the prototypes suggested power output would actually be closer to 800bhp.

The car weighed just 1000kg and was fitted with a custom-built six-speed manual transmission and clutch. Unfortunately, sprint times were never tested on the abandoned car but it was expected to achieve 62mph from standing in a little over three seconds.

SPECIFICATION

MANUFACTURE DATE	1996 - 2004	**ENGINE**	7.7-litre, 12-cylinder petrol
WIDTH	1,960 mm	**TRANSMISSION**	Six-speed manual
HEIGHT	1,130 mm	**0-62 MPH**	3.0 seconds
LENGTH	4,360 mm	**POWER OUTPUT**	1,000 / bhp (estimated)
MAXIMUM TORQUE	447 / nm	**BRAKES**	Ventilated discs, 378 mm (14.9 in) diameter (front), 273 mm (10.7 in) (rear)
MAXIMUM SPEED	240 mph	**SUSPENSION**	Double-wishbone coil springs over gas dampers, anti-roll bar

The body of the TVR 12 Speed was built from carbon fibre with Kevlar reinforcement for a lightweight but strong body in the event of accidents.

Interestingly, a single version of the TVR 12 Speed was actually sold after the brand rebuilt a prototype in 2005. The single model was sold to a specially selected driver but remains the only road-going TVR 12 Speed in existence.

The unique car is as distinctive as it is rare. The design encompasses triangular vents on the hood, small, circular lights and huge, bulging wheel arches.

The rest of the production models, some of which had already had pre-orders and deposits placed, were dismantled for parts as part of the brand's GT2 racing programme.

MCLAREN
F1

The McLaren F1 is one of the most iconic supercars of all time because of its sheer speed, advanced technology and stunning design.

Built by Formula One specialist McLaren, the car takes its name from the peak of motorsport and was regarded by many as the greatest driving machine of the 1990s.

The McLaren F1 is built using the most advanced technologies of its era. The carbon fibre body was strengthened by Kevlar and the engine, which was so hot it posed a threat to the carbon fibre body, was protected by gold as an insulator.

BMW designed and built an engine specifically for the McLaren F1. The engine is a 6.1-litre V12 engine developing 627bhp and the car itself weights just 1,062kg leading to a power-to-weight ratio of 559bhp per ton – more than a Bugatti Veyron.

As a result of the exceptional power-to-weight ratio the McLaren F1 is capable of tremendous speeds and even ten years after its launch it remained one of the fastest supercars in history.

The McLaren F1 is capable of a top speed of 240mph and its 0-62mph sprint time is 3.2 seconds. Acceleration from 0-100mph is just 6.3 seconds and 200mph takes 28 seconds.

The car is the brainchild of legendary designer Gordon Murray and features a mid-engine, rear-wheel drive layout. While the figures look daunting, McLaren has designed the car to precise specifications and it is a beautifully engineered machine.

However, all that power going to the rear wheels and the lack of an anti-roll bar means the back end is particularly difficult to control under high cornering speeds.

Drivers who master the McLaren F1 will get to enjoy
the roar of the V12 engine, whose fierce rumble is a
unique, distinctive sound that will thrill most drivers.

Inside the cabin, the McLaren F1 was better-equipped
than many supercars of its era. The car comes with
full air conditioning, electric windows and a CD player.
Other extras included titanium tool kit and specialized
luggage bags to fit the car's compact storage
compartments.

SPECIFICATION

MANUFACTURE DATE	1992-1998	**ENGINE**	BMW 6.1-litre V12 petrol
WIDTH	1,820 mm	**TRANSMISSION**	Six-speed manual
HEIGHT	1,140mm	**0-62 MPH**	3.2 seconds
LENGTH	4,287 mm	**POWER OUTPUT**	627 / bhp
MAXIMUM TORQUE	600 / nm	**BRAKES**	Unassisted, vented and cross-drilled brake discs made by Brembo
MAXIMUM SPEED	240 mph	**SUSPENSION**	Double-wishbone

KOENIGSEGG
CCX

Koenigsegg was at the forefront of a new wave of independent hypercar exotica in the Noughties, with models such as the CCX boasting massive overall horsepower, lightweight design and fearsome acceleration. Optimised for the track but reasonably usable on the road, the CCX cost over half a million dollars at launch.

CX stood for Competition Coupé X and the car amounted to a largely new one from Koenigsegg, with a new set of body parts designed to be functional as well as attractive: large air scoops and vents plus side skirts to enhance downforce were added while a glass window showed off the new CCX engine. Koenigsegg maintained that the CCX was one hypercar built to include tall drivers, though the car's overall height was only 1120mm above the tarmac.

Weight-saving is observed to vaguely ridiculous levels, with even wheels available in carbon fibre or magnesium. At the time, Koenigsegg claimed that the CCX had a lower unsprung weight than any other supercar.

The CCX engine was designed and manufactured completely in-house – another rarity among car-makers in the segment – while the engine that powered the CCX was an all-aluminium 4.7-litre twin supercharged V8 engine that could be mated to a 6-speed manual and a 6-speed automated manual gearbox and torque-sensitive limited slip differential.

Power of 795bhp and torque of 920Nm equalled stupendous performance figures. The 60mph sprint took 3.2 seconds, while hitting 124mph (200km/h) took 9.8. Sprinting to 124mpg then stopping to zero took 14 seconds dead. The CCX was aided in its performance by a lightweight construction that mixed Kevlar, carbon fibre and aluminium, while the drag coefficient was a low 0.30.

With a removable targa roof, in-house design and blistering performance – and with many modifications required to make the car viable in the USA – the CCX was a revolutionary car that launched Koenigsegg onto the world stage.

SPECIFICATION

MANUFACTURE DATE	2006-10	**ENGINE**	4.7-litre twin supercharged V8 engine
WIDTH	1,996 mm	**TRANSMISSION**	Six-speed manual or Six-speed auto
HEIGHT	1,120 mm	**0-62 MPH**	3.2 seconds
LENGTH	4,293 mm	**POWER OUTPUT**	795 / bhp
MAXIMUM TORQUE	920 / nm	**BRAKES**	Ceramic 382mm front discs with 8-piston calipers at front; 362mm with 6 piston calipers at rear
MAXIMUM SPEED	241 mph	**SUSPENSION**	Double-wishbone, two-way adjustable VPS gas-hydraulic shock absorbers, pushrod operated

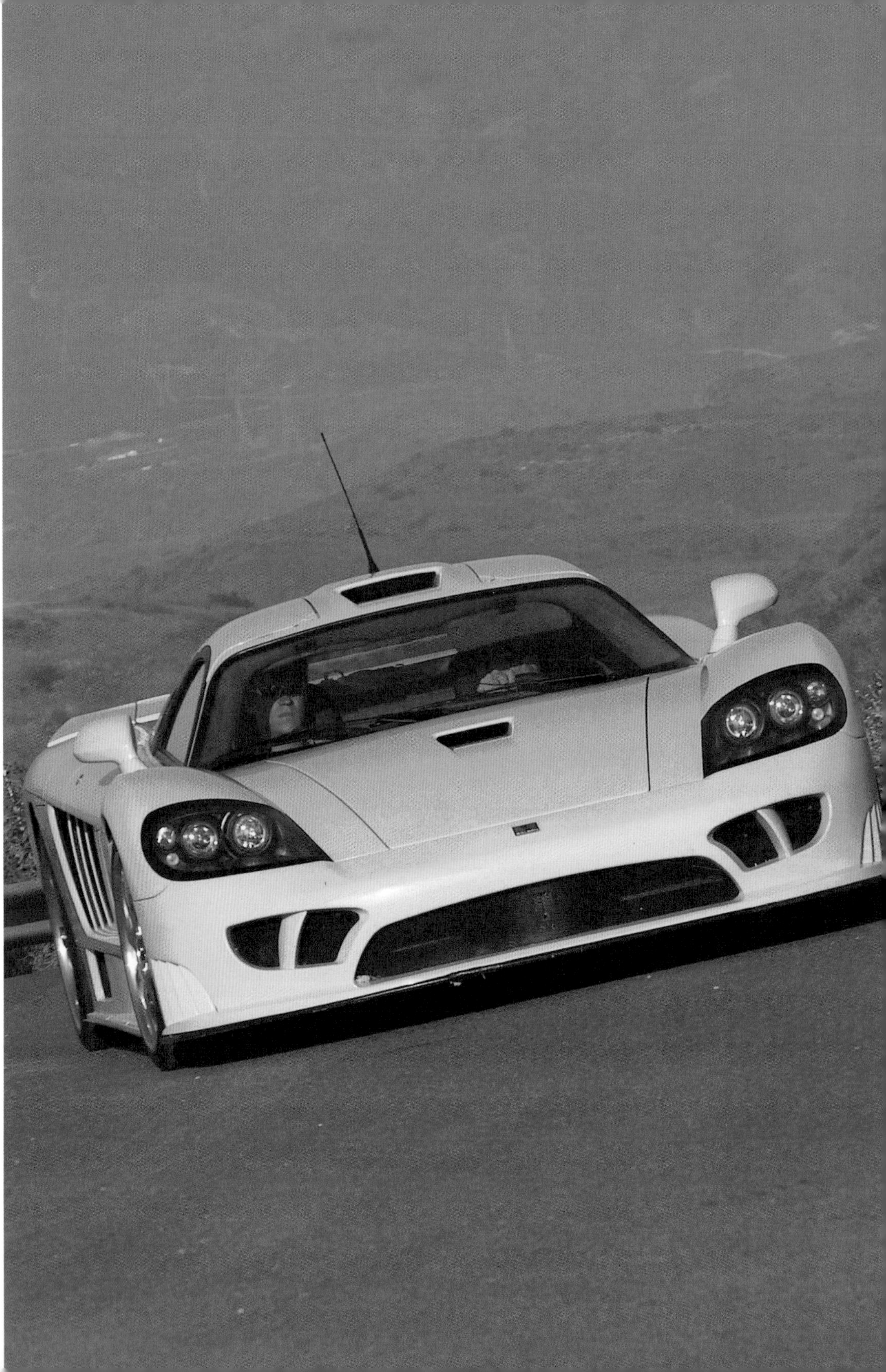

SALEEN
S7 TWIN TURBO

The Saleen S7 Twin Turbo has headline-grabbing performance statistics including a top speed of 248mph.

For a car to reach such frightening speeds it takes an incredibly powerful engine and engineering brilliance and the Saleen S7 Twin Turbo can claim to have both.

The engine is a 7.0-litre V8 originally used in the first Saleen S7 but the addition of twin turbochargers has boosted power from around 500bhp to 750bhp and 952Nm of torque at 4800rpm. Developed in-house, the engine is matched to a six-speed manual transmission.

When coupled with a kerbweight of just 1,338kg the Saleen S7 Twin Turbo delivers phenomenal performance to take the title of fastest US production car ever built.

The Saleen S7 Twin turbo can accelerate from 0-62mph in less than three seconds and goes on to hit 100mph in less than six seconds. Formidable performance calls for advanced technology and the Saleen S7 uses specially-designed Brembo brakes and diffusers and spoilers to increase down force.

The Saleen S7 Twin Turbo has its origins in Ford's most iconic car, the Mustang. Famed Mustang engineer Steve Saleen is behind the creation of the US' fastest production car and even uses a Ford NASCAR engine for his supercar.

The large brakes and power-assisted, rack-and-pinion steering are a supercar driver's dream; they enable the car to be precise around corners with sharp, corrective handling wherever necessary in order to keep the car on the road.

Striking scissor doors and a traditional, low, curvaceous supercar shape will appeal to enthusiasts almost as much as the Saleen S7's driving characteristics.

Meanwhile, the interior includes some luxury touches including leather and aluminium highlights, custom luggage as standard and a rear view camera to make up for low visibility in the rear.

The rear-wheel drive supercar is significantly less expensive than its supercar rivals, despite offering performance and torque figures that cannot be matched by some of the big players from the likes of Ferrari and Lamborghini.

So performance-oriented is the two-door supercar that a racing version, named the Saleen S7R was designed to compete in the Le Mans series.

SPECIFICATION

MANUFACTURE DATE	2005–2009	**ENGINE**	7.0-litre V8 petrol
WIDTH	1,990 mm	**TRANSMISSION**	Six-speed manual
HEIGHT	1,041 mm	**0-62 MPH**	2.9 seconds
LENGTH	4,774 mm	**POWER OUTPUT**	750 / bhp
MAXIMUM TORQUE	925 / nm	**BRAKES**	Brembo disc brakes
MAXIMUM SPEED	248 mph	**SUSPENSION**	Double-wishbone suspension with aluminium dampers and anti-roll bar

LOTEC
SIRIUS

When small German supercar manufacturer Lotec announced the Sirius would be as quick as some of the fastest cars in the world there were a few raised eyebrows.

However, the use of a Mercedes-derived 6.0-litre V12 engine taken from a Pagani Zonda enabled Lotec to push the Sirius on to a top speed of 248mph.

Not only did Lotec take the engine from one of the fastest hypercars in existence it also added two turbochargers to the engine to boost power to 1183bhp and 1320Nm of torque at 3400rpm.

The lightweight design of the Lotec, which weighs just 1280kg, means it boasts one of the most impressive power-to-weight ratios in the world at 925bhp per ton. The weight is helped by a carbon fibre body, the material used in many of the world's fastest cars because of its lightweight design and strength during impact.

Despite the top speed approaching 250mph and incredible torque, the car is slightly slower than the likes of the Bugatti Veyron to reach 62mph at 3.8 seconds.

The Lotec Sirius is a car that is sold in exceptionally small numbers worldwide. Owner Lotec is perhaps better known for improving the performance of Mercedes cars instead of venturing into the world of supercar production.

High prices and low availability mean that seeing a
Lotec Sirius on the road is extremely rare but its
distinctive strip, headlamps and wrap-around
windscreen and rear window are great styling touches.
The company is capable of producing just five cars per
year and as a result this is an extremely rare car.

Other features are taken from supercar royalty
including a six-speed manual CIMA gearbox taken
from the Pagani Zonda and the dashboard from the
Porsche 944 Turbo.

The Lotec Sirius comes with a high level of equipment
considering its hypercar performance and standard
features include air conditioning, power steering and
sports bucket seats with three-point harnesses.

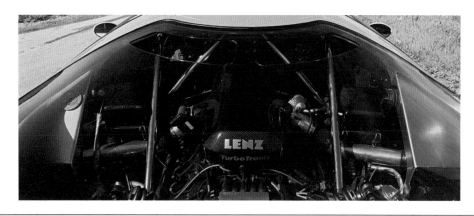

SPECIFICATION

MANUFACTURE DATE	2009	**ENGINE**	6.0-litre V12 petrol
WIDTH	2,080 mm	**TRANSMISSION**	Six-speed manual CIMA gearbox
HEIGHT	1,120 mm	**0-62 MPH**	3.8 seconds
LENGTH	4,120 mm	**POWER OUTPUT**	1,183 / bhp
MAXIMUM TORQUE	1,320 / nm	**BRAKES**	4 ram AP IMSA racing brakes
MAXIMUM SPEED	248 mph	**SUSPENSION**	Unequal-length Double-wishbone with anti-roll bar

DAUER PORSCHE
962
LE MANS

With only 13 Dauer Porsche 962 Le Mans road cars ever built it's one of the rarer supercars on the planet, though it's certainly one of the more recognisable.

O ne of a number of supercars that started life as a prototype racecar, it was developed from a stripped-down Porsche 962 chassis. The Dauer 962 Le Mans replaced some body panels with carbon fibre and Kevlar, while the underbody tray was flattened to boost stability at high speeds.

An adjustable hydraulic suspension system, a second seat, leather trim and a small luggage compartment were added to the road cars, but the cabin remained simple and smart rather than sumptuous. A video screen for DVD playback was added to later models.

The engine is a 2994cc water-cooled, twin-cam, four-valves Porsche flat-six strapped to a pair of turbochargers capable of developing 730bhp at 7,400rpm. That means from a standing start the 0-60mph sprint takes just 2.6 seconds in first gear – with double that speed taking around five seconds. The transmission used the normal 962 manual box and clutch through Tiptronic knobs on the steering wheel.

Although the Dauer Porsche 962 Le Mans was officially claimed to achieve 230 mph, there are unverified claims that the car could exceed 250 mph. At 1080kg, the 962 Le Mans has a power-to weight ratio superior to the McLaren F1 – the car was claimed to be the fastest road-legal production car in the world in the mid-90s.

SPECIFICATION

MANUFACTURE DATE	1984	**ENGINE**	2,994 cc Porsche flat 6 twin turbo
WIDTH	1,985 mm	**TRANSMISSION**	Five-speed manual RWD
HEIGHT	1,050 mm	**0-62 MPH**	2.6 seconds
LENGTH	4,650 mm	**POWER OUTPUT**	730 / bhp @ 7,400 rpm
MAXIMUM TORQUE	700 / nm @ 5,000 rpm	**BRAKES**	330mm Brembo ventilated discs with 4-piston calipers
MAXIMUM SPEED	230mph	**SUSPENSION**	Double-wishbone suspension with adjustable anti-roll bars

BUGATTI
VEYRON

The car that re-started the fastest production car cold war, the Bugatti Veyron, boasts a top speed of 253 mph, making it the fastest ever built when it hit the streets in 2006.

That the Veyron originated in the Volkswagen Group was also notable, with the title of fastest production car being tilted at by numerous examples of low-volume exotica in the years preceding the Bugatti hypercar.

The Veyron took the title from the McLaren F1 – for a long time the last word in high-speed road cars – and hung on to it until superseded by an even faster version of the same model – the Super Sport.

The Veyron outputs 987bhp and is good for a top speed of 253mph courtesy of a quad-turbocharged 8-litre WR16 with peak torque of 1250Nm developed between 2200 and 5500rpm.

Creating all that power and torque was one thing, but transmitting it to the Veyron's four wheels required a bespoke transmission, resulting in a seven-speed twin-clutch DSG gearbox operated automatically or via paddle shifters, with lightning-quick changes thanks to the presence of two clutches, one engaged and one waiting to be engaged.

Torque is split automatically depending on conditions and, at 137mph, the Veyron lowers its suspension and extends a rear spoiler to increase downforce. To push onto the top speed the driver must switch on a different driving mode that turns off these aids and ensures that tyres are undamaged. The result is decreased downforce and a slipper drag coefficient, enabling the top speed of 253mph.

To 200mph from a standing start takes 22 seconds and the standing quarter-mile a mere 10.8 seconds. The Veyron remains a technological marvel – one that doesn't offer a stripped-out interior without everyday usability but is perfectly pliable as a grand tourer – and will continue to be synonymous with the title of fastest production car.

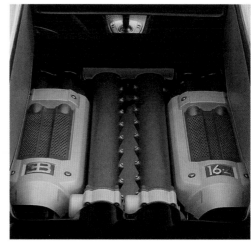

SPECIFICATION

MANUFACTURE DATE	2006–2011	**ENGINE**	Quad-turbocharged and intercooled DOHC 64-valve 7998cc W-16, aluminium block and heads, direct fuel injection
WIDTH	1,998 mm	**TRANSMISSION**	Seven-speed manual with automated shifting and clutch
HEIGHT	1,159 mm	**0-62 MPH**	2.9 seconds
LENGTH	4,462 mm	**POWER OUTPUT**	987 / bhp @ 6,000 rpm
MAXIMUM TORQUE	1,250 / nm @ 2,200 rpm	**BRAKES**	Carbon-ceramic eight-piston, four-pad calipers at front; six-piston, two-pad calipers at rear
MAXIMUM SPEED	253 mph	**SUSPENSION**	Independent Double-wishbone Front & Rear

KOENIGSEGG
CCXR

The Koenigsegg CCXR was an ultra-low-volume biofuel roadster released in 2008 with enough power and top speed to bother the Bugatti Veyron, then the official fastest production car.

T he performance statistic are quite fascinating. With a relatively small displacement 4.8-litre engine boosted by two centrifugal superchargers, the CCXR was capable of a reported 254mph, developing 1,018bhp and sprinting to 60mph in 2.9 seconds when using bioethanol. A standing start to 124mph and back again took just 13.5 seconds.

One of the secrets of the Koenigsegg hypercar is that it is clothed almost completely in lightweight carbon fibre and boasts other weight-saving trickery as an aluminium honeycomb chassis and hollow drive shafts, but the performance improvements offered by higher-octane bioethanol meant that more power could be wrung from the engine due to the higher cylinder pressures that the cooling properties of the fuel allowed.

With all that power, came the need for plenty of downforce. As a result the CCXR came with an adjustable rear wing and massive front splitter. Meanwhile, ceramic disc brakes, a limited-slip differential and five-mode traction control ensured the car stayed in contact with the tarmac.

The CCXR didn't skimp either. Leather carpets, a DVD player, satnav and a rear-view parking camera were among standard offerings. The Koenigsegg's glass roof was removable, too.

The CCXR wasn't just fast – in a world of petrol-powered coupés and as a biofuel drop-top, it offered something genuinely different.

SPECIFICATION

MANUFACTURE DATE	2007–2011	**ENGINE**	4759cc, V8 petrol / bioethanol
WIDTH	1,996 mm	**TRANSMISSION**	Six-speed sequential
HEIGHT	1,120 mm	**0-62 MPH**	2.9 seconds
LENGTH	4,293 mm	**POWER OUTPUT**	1,018 / bhp @ 7,200 rpm
MAXIMUM TORQUE	1,060 / nm @ 5,600 rpm	**BRAKES**	380mm power-assisted front ventilated ceramic disc brakes with 8-piston light alloy Brembo calipers at front; 362mm power-assisted rear ventilated ceramic disc brakes with 6-piston light alloy AP Racing calipers at rear
MAXIMUM SPEED	254mph	**SUSPENSION**	Double-wishbone, two-way adjustable VPS gas-hydraulic shock absorbers, pushrod operated

9FF
GT9

The fastest-ever Porsche-based supercar is the 9ff GT9, a coupé built by tuning company 9ff that uses the Porsche 911 997 GT3 as donor car and produces the 254mph GT9. So heavily modified from the original was the GT9 that it reputedly shared only two per cent of the same components with the 911 GT3.

The 911 GT3 body was stretched by 300mm and flattened by 120mm to maximize downforce at high speeds. Meanwhile, heavy use of carbon fibre and Kevlar meant the GT9 weighed in at a lightweight 1,326kg.

The models use a heavily-modified 4.0-litre flat-six petrol engine mounted in the middle of the car, as opposed to the traditional rear position for which the 911 is famous.

The engine is capable of developing 987bhp and a top speed of 254mph, making it faster than the Bugatti Veyron. 0-60mph took 2.9 seconds and 0-190mph less than 16 seconds.

Very much a racing car, the 911's interior was stripped out to make the GT9, with blue leather trim and a roll cage added. Neither traction control nor stability control were available with the GT9, ensuring the coupé attracted only hardcore – and well-to-do at around $800,000 – buyers.

Only 20 of the most powerful models were ever sold, making the GT9 one of the most exclusive fastest cars on the planet.

SPECIFICATION

MANUFACTURE DATE	2007–2008	**ENGINE**	4.0-litre B6 twin-turbo
WIDTH	1,860 mm	**TRANSMISSION**	Six-speed Manual
HEIGHT	1,180 mm	**0-62 MPH**	2.9 seconds
LENGTH	4,733 mm	**POWER OUTPUT**	987 / bhp
MAXIMUM TORQUE	964 / nm	**BRAKES**	Ceramic brake system; 2-piece brake discs with aluminium bells; 380mm 6-piston brake calipers at front; 350 4-piston brake calipers at rear
MAXIMUM SPEED	254 mph	**SUSPENSION**	Fully adjustable suspension with adjustable aluminium shock absorbers

BUGATTI VEYRON
16.4 GRAND SPORT VITESSE

The Bugatti Veyron 16.4 Grand Sport Vitesse
promised to unite the elegance of the Grand Sport
and the performance of the Super Sport – it remains
the fastest production roadster ever built as of 2013
and an incredible feat of engineering in its
own right.

An improved version of the eight-litre W16 engine is capable of developing maximum torque of 1,500Nm between 3,000–5,000rpm and provides maximum power of 1,184bhp at 6,400rpm.

Those awesome figures mean the Vitesse can cover the sprint in just 2.6 seconds and go on to a top speed of 255mph, with power transmitted through a new version of the 7-speed DSG dual-clutch transmission. Such is the quantity of fuel being burned at maximum speed that the waste heat from the Veyron's engine could warm ten family homes in the winter.

Powering a car to over 250mph requires a delicate balance between aerodynamic slippiness and downforce to ensure traction – the Veyron's mix of suspension settings and aerodynamic features ensures that the car is stable at 250mph.

However, removing the Veyron's roof obviously compromises this balance. As a result, the front end of the Grand Sport Vitesse is characterized by larger air intakes and the rear by a double diffuser and a centrally-positioned twin tailpipe.

Removing the roof also poses certain torsional stiffness differences, so a full carbon fibre monocoque ensures stiffness of 22,000Nm per degree. A third problem with producing a roadster capable of over 250mph is the issue of tyre and wind noise so engineers added a new, stowable, windbreak that Bugatti promised would ensure relaxed open-top driving even at a speed illegal in most countries.

That the Vitesse can manage this top speed at all is astounding. That it can do it as a roadster just makes the Veyron – already an incredible car – that much more astonishing.

SPECIFICATION

MANUFACTURE DATE	2006–2011	ENGINE	Quad-turbocharged and intercooled DOHC 64-valve 7998cc W-16, aluminium block and heads, direct fuel injection
WIDTH	1,998 mm	TRANSMISSION	Seven-speed manual with automated shifting and clutch
HEIGHT	1,159 mm	0-62 MPH	2.6 seconds
LENGTH	4,462 mm	POWER OUTPUT	1,184 / bhp
MAXIMUM TORQUE	1,500 / nm	BRAKES	Carbon-ceramic eight-piston, four-pad calipers at front; six-piston, two-pad calipers at rear
MAXIMUM SPEED	255 mph	SUSPENSION	Independent Double-wishbone Front & Rear

HENNESSEY
VENOM GT

The Hennessey Venom GT may not quite be the world's fastest production car, but it is the world's fastest accelerating production car – capable of going to 186mph (300km/h) in 13.63 seconds.

Not only that it went on to claim an unofficial 0-200mph time of 14.51 seconds – beating the likes of the Koenigsegg Agera R by over three seconds and the Bugatti Veyron by more than seven seconds. It's a fast car.

The Venom GT is hardly a slouch in the top speed stakes either; capable of 260mph it's among the elite fastest cars in the world - company founder John Hennessey claims the Venom is, in fact, the fastest production car available to the public as the Veyron's record-breaking runs have been achieved with a speed-limiter deactivated.

Powered by a 7.0-litre V8 producing 1,244 hp and 1,565Nm of torque, the two-seater, real-wheel-drive coupé weighs just 1,244kg – meaning a power-to-weight ratio of exactly one horsepower per kilogram of kerbweight.

The Venom GT is loosely based on the chassis of a Lotus Exige, with extensive modifications and various driver aids to ensure traction. A programmable traction control system manages power output, with power adjustable by the driver so that bands of 800bhp, 1000bhp and the maximum power of 1244bhp are available.

An active aero system with an adjustable rear wing deploys at very high speeds, increasing downforce, while an adjustable suspension system will allow ride height adjustments according to speed and driving conditions.

With Hennessey only planning to build 29 Venom GTs at a rate of one a year and over $1m each – not to mention with a stereo system supposedly designed by Steven Tyler of Aerosmith – the Venom GT is likely to remain a highly sought-after piece of hypercar exotica.

SPECIFICATION

MANUFACTURE DATE	2012	**ENGINE**	Chevrolet LS V8 Block 6.2 Litre with twin Garrett ball-bearing turbochargers
WIDTH	1,960 mm	**TRANSMISSION**	Ricardo Six-speed Manual
HEIGHT	1,079 mm	**0-62 MPH**	2.9 seconds
LENGTH	4,655 mm	**POWER OUTPUT**	1,244 / bhp
MAXIMUM TORQUE	1,565 / nm	**BRAKES**	Brembo 6-piston on carbon ceramic discs
MAXIMUM SPEED	260 mph	**SUSPENSION**	Type: KW Variant 3 Adjustable Coilover

KOENIGSEGG
AGERA R

The Agera R made its debut at the March 2011 Geneva Motor Show trumpeted as a supercar capable of running on biofuel – something Koenigsegg has shown in the past with the CCX.

The Agera R can accelerate from 0 to 60mph in 2.9 seconds and reach a theoretical top speed of approximately 275mph, though it is officially rated at 260mph. During testing the Agera R managed to rack up a Guinness World Records for high-speed acceleration and braking in a two-seater production car 0-300-0 km/h in 21.19 seconds.

The Koenigsegg hypercar is powered by a 1,115bhp 5.0-litre V8 twin-turbo petrol engine. Power is transmitted through a dual clutch transmission for faster gearshifts.

The Agera has a body made from pre-impregnated carbon fibre and Kevlar with lightweight reinforcements., while the chassis is made using carbon fibre with an aluminium honeycomb.

The Agera comes with forged aluminium wheels with centre locking and a set of Michelin Super Sport tyres good for 260mph. Unlike some hypercars, there's a traction control system, while the active wing on the Agera R balances downforce and aerodynamic slippiness.

It's manually or automatically adjustable – in the latter case it uses the pressure of the wind created at high speeds to force the wing downward and reduce wind resistance – meaning it is lighter than conventional hydraulics and instantly adaptable to headwinds or tailwinds.

Other highlights include the trademark Koenigsegg right-angle doors and a custom interior with Ghost Light lighting system, which uses carbon nanotubes to backlight the car's aluminium buttons. Koenigsegg claims the Agera R has the largest trunk space of any hypercar at 120 litres, where the roof can be stowed if topless driving is desired.

With those everyday touches the Agera R almost becomes a new kind of car entirely – a hypercar GT.

SPECIFICATION

MANUFACTURE DATE	2012	**ENGINE**	5.0-litre V8 with twin turbos
WIDTH	1,996 mm	**TRANSMISSION**	Seven-speed dual clutch
HEIGHT	1,120 mm	**0-62 MPH**	2.8 seconds
LENGTH	4,293 mm	**POWER OUTPUT**	1,115 / bhp
MAXIMUM TORQUE	1,200 / nm	**BRAKES**	392mm and 380mm ventilated and drilled ceramic discs
MAXIMUM SPEED	260 mph	**SUSPENSION**	Koenigsegg Triplex suspension

FAST CARS

FASTEST

CAR IN THE WORLD

BUGATTI
VEYRON SUPER SPORT

Where do you go from the fastest ever production car? If you're Bugatti you go even faster. The Veyron Super Sport was first unveiled in 2010 and immediately became the world's fastest production car, courtesy of its 267.856mph top speed.

Despite queries over the validity of the claim given the production car's speed limiter, which brings the attainable speed down to a mere 258mph, the Guinness Book of World Records still proclaims the Super Sport the fastest car in the world, as of 2013.

With a power increase to 1,188bhp, torque boost to 1,500Nm and aerodynamic tweaks, the grand tourer is capable of 267mph, but is limited to 258mph to prevent its tyres from overheating. However, it does cover the 60mph sprint in 2.5 seconds dead and 124mph (200km/h) in 6.7 seconds.

Because the sheer power required to move at those speeds through air increases exponentially with every mile-per-hour, the Super Sport will empty its 100-litre fuel tank in eight minutes when travelling at top speed, as opposed to the standard Veyron managing to burn through its fuel in 12.

The Veyron represents the very limits of our grasp of physics; sending a car that can happily admit two people and an air conditioning unit at speeds well beyond what's possible for a Formula One car.

As a mark of how difficult that is, Bugatti is believed to lose money on every Veyron it sells – the sheer weight of research and development required means an outlay of many millions of dollars.

30 will be produced at prices of over $2m. Chances are you might never even see one. The best car in the world? Perhaps. But the Bugatti Veyron Super Sports is certainly the fastest.

SPECIFICATION

MANUFACTURE DATE	2011	**ENGINE**	Quad-turbocharged and intercooled DOHC 64-valve 7998cc W-16, aluminium block and heads, direct fuel injection
WIDTH	1,998 mm	**TRANSMISSION**	Seven-speed manual with automated shifting and clutch
HEIGHT	1,159 mm	**0-62 MPH**	2.5 seconds
LENGTH	4,462 mm	**POWER OUTPUT**	1,188 / bhp
MAXIMUM TORQUE	1,500 / nm	**BRAKES**	Carbon-ceramic eight-piston, four-pad calipers at front; six-piston, two-pad calipers at rear
MAXIMUM SPEED	267 mph	**SUSPENSION**	Independent Double-wishbone Front & Rear

FAST CARS
INDEX

PICTURE CREDITS

All images copyright of Evo Mawhing Ltd.